Michel Foucault's Practical Philosophy

SUNY series in Contemporary French Thought

David Pettigrew and François Raffoul, editors

Michel Foucault's Practical Philosophy

A Critique of Subjectivation Processes

Maddalena Cerrato

Translated by Stefano Franchi

Cover Credit: Pair of Standing Nude Male Figures Demonstrating the Principles of Contrapposto according to Michelangelo and Phidias, Auguste Rodin, ca. 1911
Published by State University of New York Press, Albany
© 2025 State University of New York
All rights reserved
Printed in the United States of America

No part of this book may be used or reproduced in any manner whatsoever without written permission. No part of this book may be stored in a retrieval system or transmitted in any form or by any means including electronic, electrostatic, magnetic tape, mechanical, photocopying, recording, or otherwise without the prior permission in writing of the publisher.

Links to third-party websites are provided as a convenience and for informational purposes only. They do not constitute an endorsement or an approval of any of the products, services, or opinions of the organization, companies, or individuals. SUNY Press bears no responsibility for the accuracy, legality, or content of a URL, the external website, or for that of subsequent websites.

EU GPSR Authorised Representative:
Logos Europe, 9 rue Nicolas Poussin, 17000, La Rochelle, France
contact@logoseurope.eu

For information, contact State University of New York Press, Albany, NY
www.sunypress.edu

Library of Congress Cataloging-in-Publication Data

Names: Cerrato, Maddalena, author.
Title: Michel Foucault's practical philosophy : a critique of
  subjectivation processes / Maddalena Cerrato ; translated by Stefano
  Franchi.
Description: Albany : State University of New York Press, [2025] | Series:
  SUNY series in contemporary French thought | Includes bibliographical
  references and index.
Identifiers: LCCN 2024042828 | ISBN 9798855802207 (hardcover) | ISBN
  9798855802221 (ebook) | ISBN 9798855802214 (paperback)
Subjects: LCSH: Foucault, Michel, 1926–1984.
Classification: LCC B2430.F724 C4513 2025 | DDC 194—dc23/eng/20241202
LC record available at https://lccn.loc.gov/2024042828

To my mother, in memoriam

Contents

Foreword to the English Edition and Acknowledgments, ix

Introduction, 1

1. Practical Philosophy as the Horizon of Foucault's Thought, 19

2. Power, Biopower, Governmentality, 39

3. The Christian Model: Pastoral Care and Government of Truth, 65

4. Subjectivation Processes and the Task of Philosophy, 81

Afterword: The Legacy of Foucault's Practical Philosophy, 107

Notes, 111

Bibliography, 125

Index, 133

Foreword to the English Edition and Acknowledgments

Today, June 25, 2024, marks exactly forty years from Michel Foucault's death. The *Collège de France* decided to honor the occasion by starting the public release of some of the lecture course recordings that were the object of the editing work that Seuil-Gallimard fully accomplished in 2015. However, finding myself in front of the computer screen to write these last remarks intended to accompany the English edition of my book *Michel Foucault's Practical Philosophy* on the day of this anniversary is an uncanny coincidence, rather than a planned tribute to the thinker to whom I dedicated the formative years of my doctorate. Even more uncanny is realizing the coincidence by noticing the multiple recurrences of the *Collège de France*'s announcement while scrolling through my social media feed, that is, precisely in the act of searching for a way to slide into mindless avoidance of the difficult engagement with this work and its meaning. The social media post, unsurprisingly shared by so many of my professional contacts and friends, provided a very timely reminder that this further attempt to avoid dealing with the theoretical and existential implications of my inquiry into Michel Foucault's work was nothing but the last of a series of deferments responsible for the significant lapse of time between the Italian edition of the book and this publication. It was almost exactly fifteen years ago when, at the end of the first year of my PhD, I went to the IMEC (Institut Mémoires de l'Édition Contemporain) in Caen and, listening from the Foucault Archive to some of those same recordings whose public release was announced today, I found the excitement and the spirit of inquiry that helped me take the first clumsy and necessary steps of my academic career.

The task of confronting the self-critical questions concerning this work, its inscription in the historical condition of my thinking, and, of course, its projection into the ideal space of the field of Foucauldian studies is not an easy one. And yet, one of the most important lessons I have learned from Foucault is certainly never to forget to consider the practical and historical dimension of thinking, to submit your own thought to the same genealogical problematization to which one submits philosophical literature, and never underestimate how the exercise of philosophy takes place through multiple distinct experiences of thinking, writing, and engaging critically with the present.

Over its life-span, this project has gone through multiple stages, periods of abandonment, and revisions, but it also quietly shaped the direction that my work took thereafter. Despite the challenge of accepting the difference in tone and style of the writer I was and the inevitable impulse of rewriting, I limited myself to a few cosmetic changes and updates, and to adding just a few conclusions, since the argument and substantial contribution of the book continue to be relevant. The responsibility for all that follows is exclusively mine, and yet, many people played different important roles throughout this long gestation that is coming to an end. First, I must thank professors Pietro Montani and Alberto Moreiras, to whom I am bound by an immeasurable intellectual debt, for all the trust, guidance, and encouragement they have given me during my PhD and beyond. I met Pietro Montani during my first semester in college and attending his magnetic lectures I learned the pleasure of rigorous close reading, discovered the works of Martin Heidegger, and was confirmed in my desire to study philosophy. I soon began to rely on his mentorship and support. I am grateful for the individualized challenges he offered to me over the years and for teaching me to love academic writing. The encounter with Alberto Moreiras, on the occasion of the intensive seminar he taught at the Istituto Italiano di Scienze Umane in Naples, turned out to be life-changing in many ways. His enthusiasm and intellectual creativity have been an incredible motivating force over more than a decade. The depth of my professional gratitude to him as a mentor is matched only by the profound friendship that binds us. I am thankful for all his generous feedback, the stimulating philosophical conversations, and his unwavering optimism in creating always new spaces for discussions and reading groups, as much as I am thankful for having shared the warm company of his family during uncountable holiday meals.

From the years of my PhD and the preparation of the Italian manuscript of the book, I want to thank Jorge Alvarez Yagüez for the lively Foucauldian discussions, Liliana Rampello for her precious help in the revision phase, Giacomo Marramao for the availability he has so often demonstrated, Roberto Esposito and the SUM (now part of the Scuola Normale) for supporting my research activity, Michela Russo and Peter Baker for their friendship, and my family, without whose help none of this would have ever happened.

I am very grateful to the IMEC for the access to the Foucault archives, and for the incredibly inspiring atmosphere of the Abbaye d'Ardenne and the uniquely formative experience of archival work, for which the convenience of online access to digital materials could never be a substitute — yet granting that open public access is extremely important. I am thankful to the Bush School of Government and Public Policy at Texas A&M University for granting me funding through the book subvention program, and to Michael Rinella and SUNY Press for their prompt support at every stage of the publication process.

Finally, this book would have never been published in English if not for the energetic encouragement of Adam Rosenthal and Sergio Villalobos-Ruminott, and for the support of Dinah Hannaford, Humberto José González Nuñez, Jaime Rodriguez Matos, Teresa Vilarós Soler, and Gareth Williams. I want to thank Stefanie Harris for having been a generous mentor, an inspiring colleague and department head, and for continuing to be my friend. I am grateful to Stefano Franchi for the impeccable translation of my work, and to James Martell, Sergio Villalobos-Ruminott, and Peter Baker for their incredibly valuable feedback. I want to thank Kurt Sernett for helping with the editing of the manuscript and Rockney Reid for his work on the index. I am thankful to my collogues Rob Carley, Wendi Kaspar, Robert Shandley, and John Schuessler for their guidance and support, and to Carmela Garritano for her comradeship during the time of our transition to a new department and for her continuous caring mentorship. My gratitude and love to Rick Curry for his patient reading and help editing my work over and over, and for his steadfast partnership that makes everything possible.

Introduction

The scope of Michel Foucault's work goes well beyond the analysis of modern modes of power. It is more broadly and fundamentally concerned with the problematization of subjectivation processes and the ways they are fundamentally intertwined with multiple registers of power. By proposing the interpretative framework of *practical philosophy*, this book engages holistically with Foucault's thought, and it accounts for his original approach to the exercise of philosophy and critique as active experiences of freedom, resistance, and emancipation.

After the publication of his 1986 book *Foucault*, Gilles Deleuze explains in these words to his interviewer the choice of writing a comprehensive work on Foucault despite having already published several essays on specific aspects of his thought:

> Here I'm trying to see Foucault's thought as a *whole*. By the whole, I mean what drives him on from one level of things to another: what drives him to discover power behind knowledge, and what drives him to discover "modes of subjectivation" beyond the confines of power. The logic of someone's thought is the whole set of crises through which it passes; it's more like a volcanic chain than a stable system close to equilibrium. I wouldn't have felt the need to write this book if I hadn't had the impression that people didn't really understand these transitions, this pushing forward, this logic in Foucault. (Deleuze 1995, 84)

Following the logic of a thought that is not "a stable system close to equilibrium," but rather "a wind blowing us on, a series of gusts and jolts" (1995, 94) was the aim that guided Deleuze, and it is the focus of this book as well. After almost thirty years, Deleuze's words still provide a perfect answer to the question this book is bound to prompt: why write yet another general, nonexhaustive study on a thinker who has already received so much critical attention?

Like for Deleuze, my main concern is still how to do justice to a thought whose inner logic may only be grasped by tracing its irregular and discontinuous movements, and by charting all its crises, jolts, and slips, which, however, do not ever get to properly constitute radical *turns*. And this concern is inseparable from the critical need to confront the weakness of those interpretations that either misunderstood the significance of those shifts or tried to ignore them altogether, especially now that such interpretations have accumulated over the last thirty-five years and have become part of a sort of Foucauldian common sense. The most widespread of those misinterpretations holds that Foucault's path underwent a radical turn toward the end of the 1970s, when he allegedly abandoned the political dimension of his previous work and returned to the subject through the adoption of a solipsistic ethical perspective. The widely accepted cliché of *a turn* in his thought is at the root of the alleged interpretative enigma that hangs over the last few years of Foucault's research. Like the proverbial blankets that always end up being too short and leave something exposed, such interpretations tend to shortchange the last phase of Foucault's thought. Thus, I contend that to grasp the *logic of Foucault's thought* as it emerges from the various crises and adjustments, we first need to abandon the assumption that it underwent an "ethical turn." On the other hand, such a goal also requires finding a perspective capable of matching the dynamism of Foucault's thinking and the broad scope of his research, rather than being simply directed at capturing them within a preestablished order of philosophical discourse. A new critical approach is necessary to understand the novelty of Foucault's critical proposal and to avoid forcing the dynamic logic guiding his thought into rigid preestablished categories unsuitable to account for it, as well as to avoid contenting oneself with barely mapping, either chronologically or thematically, his itinerary. *Practical philosophy* offers a direct access to the core of Foucault's thought and a new critical perspective on the general meaning of his philosophical project and its, all but linear, diachronic development. If Deleuze's 1986 book was "trying to see Foucault's thought as a whole" to account for "what drives [Foucault] on from one level of things to another," and for the logic that grounds "the whole set of crises through which it passes" (1995, 84), this book aims to show also that the importance of understanding such a logic goes beyond the need of an overarching interpretative horizon accounting for the meaning of different phases of Foucault's thought. What is at stake is the chance to assess the import of Foucault's "philosophical project" as an overcoming of the philosophy of the subject and the separation between theory and historicity. The expression *practical philosophy* refers to this project, and Foucault's legacy must be assessed against it.

Early Reception

As Alessandro Fontana (2008) pointed out, Foucault has now been officially canonized. His thought has encountered a transversal massive process of cannibalization and popularization alongside an interpretive standardization. The alleged accessibility of Foucault's texts has oftentimes encouraged trivial misuses of decontextualized concepts and loose fragments of his work. The criticisms and controversies his thought was raising until the 1980s have become progressively weaker, and he has now earned the status of a fundamental, universally recognized philosopher. And yet, it still seems able to generate new controversies, as the recent polemics initiated by the unsubstantiated and quickly debunked accusations of sexual abuses included in Guy Sorman's *Dictionnaire du bullshit* and taken up by the *Sunday Times* in April 2021 have shown.[1]

In the common imaginary, Foucault is associated with the French movements of May 1968 and he is held essentially as a political thinker whose philosophical research culminated in the relational theory of power and in the development of the concepts of biopower and biopolitics. Such a mainstream representation underwrites the idea that an "ethical turn" took place in Foucault's late thought as the result of a theoretical checkmate. An alleged failure in the field of political theory is supposed to have prompted Foucault's desire to move toward a more intimate and spiritual dimension of thought to escape the dangers of a biopolitical society. Unable to develop the relational paradigm of power into a systematic theory providing a fully articulated account of biopolitics, Foucault would have been prompted toward a retreat into the intimate subjective dimension of ethical reflections. As I have suggested, it is imperative to clear the ground from these interpretive commonplaces as they constitute the most misleading misunderstanding of the dynamics, the shifts, and internal goals of Foucault's work not because of some sterile philological urge, but rather to be able to problematize and advance a critical assessment of the legacy of his thought.

Here I decided to take as the reference point for my critical stance the book *Michel Foucault: Beyond Structuralism and Hermeneutics* written in 1982 by the American scholars Hubert Dreyfus and Paul Rabinow — which is the first and, most likely, still the most important monograph on Foucault's thought. Two elements motivated my choice. First, Dreyfus and Rabinow's interpretation is a milestone of Foucauldian criticism, laying out, implicitly and explicitly, the main guidelines that constrained the ensuing debate on his philosophical legacy, as well as its misunderstanding. Second, their book includes as an afterword the then unpublished Foucauldian essay titled "The Subject and Power" (1982): a text that constitutes one of Foucault's most punctual and complete efforts to elucidate the overall sense of his research by tying it to the issue of the subject. While the inclusion of "The Subject and Power" in Dreyfus and Rabinow's book represents from the part of Foucault an endorsement and a tribute to the years of collaboration at Berkeley, it also implied that some of the most important ideas therein included fell prey to the same misunderstandings that conditioned the reception of the rest of his work, starting with the statement, "Thus, it is not power, but the subject, which is the general theme of my research" (209). In contrast with Dreyfus and Rabinow's approach, throughout the book I take Foucault's suggestions concerning the role of the issue of the subject at face value and I turn to it to account for the logic of a thought that, while never aspiring to be systematic, followed a definite direction that guided it through the crises and necessary conceptual adjustments that no original philosophical reflection can actually ever avoid.

In a 2008 essay titled "The Non-Existent Subject" [*Il soggetto che non c'è*], Pier Aldo Rovatti underscores the still outstanding need for a thorough understanding of Foucault's thinking and the importance that such an interpretative work would have for the contemporary philosophical debate:

> A work of excavation that would dig deep within Michel Foucault's thought and theoretical praxis. As far as I can see, the interpreters have not tackled this task yet, or they have barely glimpsed at it. The material needed for this work is now finally available, and the research itself would have a particular relevance to the politico-philosophical debate. At least, it would clear out several misunderstandings and ambiguities that Foucault's legacy — an analytical tool that can no longer be underestimated — is still harboring. (Rovatti 2008, 116)

As Rovatti notices, while the early critics only had access to his published books,[2] today scholars finally have access to the needed material to accomplish such a comprehensive work of excavation and dissipate the misunderstandings that are surrounding Foucault's thought. Nonetheless, in the years immediately following his death some distinguished interpreters, who had already paid attention to his many self-reflective statements, produced readings whose far-sightedness and analytical lucidity are still unparalleled. I am referring in particular to Deleuze's and Reiner Schürmann's writings, both published in 1986, whose main interpretive direction is also implicitly inspiring Rovatti's cited essay, among others.[3] Indeed, my reading is explicitly indebted to both thinkers, and it shares their foregrounding of the concept of *subjectivation* in Foucault's thought. So, the choice to open each chapter with a quote by Deleuze signals my wish to keep open the confrontation with both authors throughout my itinerary.

As an example of an early particularly forward-looking interpretation of Foucault's perspective, one could also cite a 1985 text by François Ewald, Annette Farge, and Michelle Perrot, "Une pratique de la verité": "Michel Foucault, in particular, is not a theoretician of power, [. . .] Foucault meant to show that power and repression, state and civil society, are the most inadequate concepts to think modernity. More positively, Foucault's philosophy of truth seeks to examine the procedures through which the subject constitutes itself, or is it constituted by itself and by others" (1995, 12–13). The essay highlights very clearly the philosophical scope of Foucault's project and how it is concealed by those interpreters who read it in terms of "sociology of modernity, description of the modes of exercise of power and their effects after the classical age: genealogy and development of biopower" (1995, 13).

Across the critical bibliography, one often finds two relevant methodological observations that cannot be ignored when it comes to answering Deleuze's question about the logic of Foucault's thought. First, one should always listen to Foucault when he interprets himself; second, the various forms taken by his thought, the disparate interventions, and multiple traces of his philosophical actions are all integral components of his work. These observations do more than merely direct a fruitful approach to Foucault. They clue us in to the fact that the novelty Foucault introduces, and which makes his philosophical legacy worthy of attention, concerns his own philosophical praxis, that is, his way of *doing* philosophy. Self-interpretation and the retrospective need to interrogate one's own work are unavoidable components of Foucault's mode of thinking. As Derrida points out, "With its reflexive vigilance and care in thinking itself in its rigorous specificity, such an analysis thus calls for the problematization of its own problematization. This latter must itself also question itself, and with the same archaeological and genealogical care, the same care that it itself methodically prescribes" (1994, 264). This way of *doing* philosophy always implies a problematization of its own hermeneutic categories and demands a constant reorientation of the critical gaze. Most importantly, it compels the interpreter to consider this very conception of philosophy, as well as of its task and tools, as the horizon of sense of the accomplished philosophical work to be analyzed. In short, it requires the interpreter to move within the hermeneutic circle that binds the development of Foucault's thought to the project of a *practical philosophy*. Such a circle decides how this work unfolds, similarly to how the circularity between thought formation and thinking practices, or between historical singularities and problematizations, decides the discontinuous unfolding of Foucault's thought — the thought that Gilles Deleuze deemed "volcanic," and that Thomas Flynn described as a "spiral," when he stressed its need to continuously turn the critical gaze back upon itself (1985, 532).

Based on such methodological principles and of the important insights offered by Deleuze and Schürmann, *Michel Foucault's Practical Philosophy* tries to accomplish that *excavation work* into the rich materials available today with the aim of finding an additional answer, a further link still missing in the interpretations of my interlocutors and yet indispensable to grasp the significance of Foucault's legacy. Both Deleuze and Schürmann miss it because they fail to attend to the circularity of the relation between the critical work and its self-problematization, that is, between the philosophical questions and the question about philosophy as praxis. Both find, to use Deleuze's own words, the *logic* guiding the troubled path of Foucault's thought, and both shed light upon the underlying consistency that avoids the misunderstanding of an alleged "ethical turn." However, neither manages to provide an account of the *whole* that is always at stake to some extent throughout Foucault's philosophical itinerary.[4] Deleuze writes of "a strange three-dimensional figure, as well as the greatest of modern philosophies (and I say this without joking)," yet he gives no synoptical description (1995, 93). The missing answer concerns the specificity of Foucault's proposal, that is, his *practical philosophy*, considered as an alternative to the philosophy of the subject and as the positively characterized possibility of leaving "the philosophy of the subject" that would steer clear of structuralism's as well as of analytic philosophy's options.

Foucault's Philosophical Itinerary and Corpus

Fontana shares some important guidance on how to approach the Foucauldian corpus to avoid falling into its mystification:

> First precaution: never disjoin, never disassociate the courses, books, and the lines of actualization, as Deleuze called them, which are the multiple interventions collected in *Dits et écrits*. The courses at the Collège de France were the laboratory, the moment of fusion of thought, the incandescent phase, the thought in its constitution and in its first movement; many courses have never merged into books, or only in part. The books represent a sort of sedimentation, the taking shape of thought after the experimental phase; the speeches, the scattered articles and interviews (Foucault was undoubtedly the most interviewed philosopher of the postwar period, as if he held a word of truth, a sort of indispensable oracularity), constitute the outlets and the extension of thought and work on the present, on the actuality, on the immediate. (2008, 13)[5]

The French title of Hubert Dreyfus and Paul Rabinow's monograph *Michel Foucault, un parcours philosophique: au-delà de l'objectivité et de la subjectivité* ["Michel Foucault, a philosophical path: beyond objectivity and subjectivity"][6] suggests one should look at Foucault's work as a path. It is the path built from his books, from the courses and seminars he held during his career as a professor, from the interviews, and finally, from occasional writings that were strongly connected to the historical-political conjuncture. To understand the complexity of his itinerary then, one must follow a path that winds through four elements each as different from the other as earth, water, air, and fire: the traditional elements of pre-Socratic philosophy. All these elements must be taken into account and accounted for from their specific characteristics and the function they played in the development of Foucauldian thought.

First, there are the published books. They often represent the exclusive or, at any rate, the main referent for the interpretations of the Foucault's ideas, especially before the publication of *Dits et écrits* (1994) and the courses at the *Collège de France*, which began in 1997 with "Il faut défendre la société" and reached its completion with "Théories et institutions pénales" in 2015. Compared with the fluid experimentation of the lecture courses, which represent research as it flows (to use the metaphor of the four elements), the books are the solid result of a sedimentation of the themes and questions that emerged during the cycles of lessons, a stabilization and complete formalization of some of the problems that emerged there and, at times, were only sketched out. On the other hand, the matter that the books shaped and modeled into solid forms is the very experience of thought as it measures itself with a problem, rather than the result of a selection of material previously discussed and already presented in another form — namely, that of teaching. Foucault himself gave an apt description of this characteristic of his books in a 1978 interview with Duccio Trombadori:

> What I think is never quite the same, because for me my books are experiences, in a sense, that I would like to be as full as possible. An experience is something that one comes out of transformed. If I had to write a book to communicate what I'm already thinking before I begin to write, I would never have the courage to begin. I write a book only because I still don't exactly know what to think about this thing I want so much to think about, so that the book transforms me and transforms what I think. Each book transfers what I was thinking when I was finishing the previous book. I am an experimenter and not a theorist. I call a theorist someone who constructs a general system, either deductive or analytical, and applies it to different fields in a uniform way. That isn't my case. I'm an experimenter in the sense that I write in order to change myself and in order not to think the same thing as before. (Foucault 2001c, 240–41)

Foucault's books' experiments are content-oriented as much as they are methodological: they are not just the structuring and theoretical elaboration of issues that had emerged in other contexts. They are even less an application of preestablished methods to new contents. The search for a method of analysis is part of the experimental character of the books. This is not because Foucault does not have his own methodological tools, but rather because these tools must be questioned, forged, and tested in the course of each specific experience of thought provided by each book. As Foucault clarifies in the interview cited above, in some cases — for instance, *The Archaeology of the Human Sciences* — it was a retrospective methodological reflection that constituted the experience of thought he decided to address.[7]

Secondly, the lecture courses are the fluid element of Foucault's philosophical path. They convey the image of a thought in constant movement more than the published works do. They follow the feverish and certainly nonlinear course of his research and allow us to grasp his thought as it unfolds. Precisely for this reason, they are an invaluable tool when we try to capture the specificity of Foucauldian thought and follow the genesis of a given problematic. However, the epistemological status of the lectures is rather complex.[8] In fact, the texts of the courses give us an important part of Foucault's philosophical work, testifying as much to its contents as to how it was actually exercised. On the other hand, the transcription form seems to betray, at least in part, the very *liquid* nature of a word meant to foster teaching. In their petrified form as texts,[9] the lessons lack the tension that arose when the verbalization of thought and its exposure to a rather large group of silent interlocutors generated its own scrutiny. As we shall see in chapter 4, we lose the urgency of the link between the exercise of philosophy and actuality, in the fullest sense of the term, that characterizes Foucault's itinerary as a whole.

The third element to consider is the set of numerous interviews given by Foucault throughout his career. They undoubtedly represent the gaseous stage of Foucault's thought, marked as they are by the form of orality, the aerial character of the conversation, and the bond with the interlocutor implied by their dialogical structure. They clearly lack the philosophical rigor of the books and of the always meticulously prepared lectures. Yet even the interviews play a fundamental role in Michel Foucault's philosophical path, and they provide an essential contribution to its decoding. A first indication of their specific function comes from the aforementioned 1978 interview with Trombadori:

> I also put forward some thoughts on method in articles and interviews. These tend to be reflections on a finished book that may help me to define another possible project. They are something like a scaffolding that serves as a link between a work that is coming to an end and another one that's about to begin. But this is not to state a general method that would be definitively valid for others or for myself. What I've written is never prescriptive either for me or for others — at most it's instrumental and tentative. (Foucault 2001c, 240)

The interviews inaugurate a space dedicated to self-interpretation that was only partially exhausted by methodological reflections. It is important to examine them as part of Foucault's work[10] and consider them critically, beginning with the occasions that prompted them. They give us a precious and inexhaustible set of interpretive keys to trace the different moments, successive phases of elaboration, and more or less significant adjustments and shifts that have determined the course of Foucault's path.

The fourth and last element is represented by all the articles and interventions that have been collected, together with the interviews, in the *Dits et écrits*. On the one hand, the explicit and direct link with the present makes these texts connected to the interviews. On the other, the absence of the reflexive character and the dialogical element marks a profound difference. I have associated these occasional writings with the element of fire because they highlight how current events may trigger philosophical elaborations by conveying the significance of a particular problem or field of inquiry. In this sense, we may see Foucault's interventions as the philosopher's first response to the urgency of the current situation that draws his attention to a specific phenomenon. In many cases, the response was bound to become the energetic nucleus that set in motion the action of thought as it went through the different stages already mentioned. These texts incorporate the idea that the task of the intellectual, or of the philosopher, does not lie in addressing political issues as much as in elaborating a critique of those areas and practices that "pose problems to politics" (Foucault 1997a, 327). The elaboration of the specific meaning of this critical task leads Foucault, in the 1980s, to assign a central role to the concept of *problematization*. I examine in detail this interpretation of philosophy and of the role of the philosopher in chapter 4.

Thus, we must consider the interviews, articles, and lecture courses an integral part of Foucault's production. In particular, we must consider them as that part in which Foucault's thought comes into direct contact with the *dehors*, as well as that part in which he explicitly questions the philosopher's relationship to the outside. Foucault's relationship with the *dehors* is complex and characterized by a constant tension between theoretical-philosophical reflection and political activism. He tried to gather both in the figure of the "specific intellectual"[11] who, contrary to the intellectual carrying universal values, seeks, ". . . apart from any totalization — which would be at once abstract and limiting — to open up problems that are as concrete and general as possible, problems that approach politics from behind and cut across societies on the diagonal, problems that are at once constituents of our history and constituted by that history" (Foucault 1984, 376).

On the one hand, as mentioned above, the impulse to start a series of historical-genealogical researches, such as those conveyed in *Discipline and Punish*, came from some militant experiences, such as the experience of the GIP (*Groupe d'information sur les prisons*) between 1970 and 1973. On the other hand, sometimes his analyses experienced a process of simplification and instrumental appropriation by militant groups, in which Foucault took part only occasionally and tangentially. In any case, his more or less direct involvement in the activism of the 1970s antagonist movements made him well aware of the inevitability of a certain simplified and, in some cases, mystifying use of his work. This is why a continuous work of rectification and clarification always accompanied his research. Although he liked to think of his analyses as a *boîte à outils*, a toolbox whose eventual revolutionary or conservative use is yet unknown, Foucault added an important clarification in a 1976 conversation with Los Angeles students:

> It doesn't mean that we are simply to make beautiful, or useful, or funny tools and then choose which ones to put on the market in case somebody wants to buy them or use them. All that is fine, but there is more to it than that. If you are trying to do something, for example, to make an analysis or formulate a theory, you have to know clearly how you want it to be used, for what purposes you want to make use of the tool you are building up — you — and how you want your tools to relate to the others which are being fashioned just now. So that I think the relations between the present conjunctive [sic] situation and what you are doing in a theoretical framework is very important. (Foucault 1978a, 21)

This clarification contrasts sharply with the presumed legitimacy that the reference to the expression *boîte à outils* would guarantee to any indiscriminate and decontextualized use of Foucauldian analyses. However, the need to clarify the sense of one's own research, clearing the field from all misunderstandings and especially from all its unduly attributed labels, is also an exercise of autonomy from the constraints of the cultural debate.[12] Autonomy is a necessary condition of the praxis of philosophy considered as "the displacement and transformation of frameworks of thinking, the changing of received values and all the work that has been done to think otherwise, to do something else, to become other than what one is" (Foucault 1997a, 327). If it is true, as Arnold Davidson claims, that "Foucault is usually his own best interpreter," (1986, 221) this is due, then, to the very meaning he attributed to philosophical work: "But, then, what is philosophy today — philosophical activity, I mean — if it is not the critical work that thought brings to bear on itself? In what does it consist, if not in the endeavor to know how and to what extent it might be possible to think differently, instead of legitimating what is already known?" (Foucault 1990, 2:8–9).

Déplacement vs. *Kehre*

A series of crises punctuate Foucault's philosophical journey, as it emerges from books, lectures, interviews, and occasional writings, and each crisis is marked by significant conceptual and methodological shifts [*déplacements*]. As the following chapters show, not only can these shifts be reconciled within the substantial continuity of Foucault's research, but one may even say that these shifts and crises are what constitute and guarantee the continuity and coherence of Foucault's thought, rather than calling it into question — this, of course, only as long as one understands such a continuity as the movement of thought along an articulated philosophical itinerary, rather than as the stability of a system. As the Deleuze interview cited at the beginning of this introduction suggests, this is "the logic of a thought lies in the totality of the crises it goes through." Foucault himself, during the 1979 to 1980 course at the *Collège de France*, confided to his audience:

> For me theoretical work — and I am not in any way saying this out of pride or vanity, but rather with a profound sense of my inability — does not consist in establishing and fixing the set of positions on which I would stand and the supposedly coherent link between which would form a system. My problem, or the only theoretical work that I feel is possible for me, is leaving the trace, in the most intelligible outline possible, of the movements by which I am no longer at the place where I was earlier. Hence, if you like, this constant need, or necessity, or desire to plot, so to speak, the points of passage at which each displacement risks resulting in the modification, if not of the whole curve, then at least of the way in which it can be read

and grasped in terms of its possible intelligibility. This plotting, consequently, should never be read as the plan of a permanent structure. It should not be subject to the same requirements as those imposed on a plan. Once again, it is a matter of a line of displacement, that is to say not of a line of a theoretical structure, but of the displacement by which my theoretical positions continually change. (Foucault 2016b, 76)

On several occasions, Foucault himself suggested the idea of the mobile continuity of a thought that constantly returns upon itself to redraw its itinerary, that is always ready to question its trajectory, and that adjusts its goals as it lets the experience of research modify its path even substantially. This is the idea that should guide the reading of his philosophy.

When asked to give an account of the specificity of the last phase of Foucauldian thought, and of the radical change that invested the project of *The History of Sexuality*, most interpreters resort instead — although, often only implicitly — to what we could call "the way of the *Kehre* [turning point]." This expression[13] recalls the controversial issue that animated the philosophical debate around Heidegger's thought since the publication of "Letter on Humanism" (1947). The expression has generated a hermeneutic *topos* that has somehow helped the production of an interpretative misunderstanding, of which the last phase of Foucault's thought has long remained a victim. The philosophical event that definitively marked the concept of turning point as a philosophical interpretive model is the declaration in which Heidegger confesses that, on the one hand, *Being and Time* remained incomplete "because thought could not adequately say adequately this turning point [*Kehre*] and did not come to terms with it with the help of the language of metaphysics," (1998, 250) and, on the other hand, that thought has subsequently managed to overcome the impasse and achieve the philosophical turning point to which it aspired. The concept of turning point introduced into philosophical critique by the interminable *querelle* following Heidegger's declaration seems to point to a radical change in a thinker's philosophical perspective following an impasse, or a checkmate suffered just when the research was approaching its apex. As I suggested above, the idea that Foucault experienced a "turning point" of this nature around 1980 represents the greatest obstacle to the possibility of outlining an interpretative framework capable of shedding light on the meaning of the diverse research projects of his last years — including those that are conveyed in the last three volumes of *The History of Sexuality* — with respect to the totality of Foucault's philosophical itinerary. We cannot deny the changes and the evolution that intervened in Foucault's thought, nor can we omit the possible identification of phases and crises. And yet, we must grasp the matrix of coherence that underlies the various theoretical shifts, and we must focus on all the smaller conceptual shifts rather than collapsing them into a single radical upheaval. As Deleuze puts it, we need to acknowledge that, "[a]s with all great thinkers, his thought always developed through crises and abrupt shifts that were the mark of its creativity, the mark of its ultimate consistency" (1995, 83).

Hubert Dreyfus and Paul Rabinow wrote the first and most important monograph on the thought of Michel Foucault in 1982 (1st edition). The first part of their book traces a very lucid analysis of the difficult balance of seduction and distancing that characterized, especially in the first phase of his itinerary, Foucault's relationships with structuralism, phenomenology, and Heideggerian hermeneutic ontology. The authors read both the crisis of the archaeological method and its subordination to the genealogical perspective in light of this complex relationship. Foucault's eventual philosophical destination would have consisted in a proposal that they examine mainly from a methodological perspective and define as *an interpretative analytics* of the modern subject or as "a pragmatically oriented, historical interpretation" (1982, 120). Foucault would have elaborated this method to arrive, through an analysis of power, at a diagnosis of the present centered on biopower. The concept of biopower, they argue, was born in opposition to the repressive hypothesis in which power and truth played against each other. It is "an alternative synthesis" (1982, 128) of the relationships between truth, power, sex, body, and individuals. In Dreyfus and Rabinow's reading, biopower is the culmination of the Foucauldian *parcours philosophique*. The idea of the mutual determination of power and knowledge — which "is one of Foucault's major contributions" (1982, 203) — is linked here to "one of Foucault's major achievements" (1982, 112), namely, the conceptualization of how the body became a constitutive element of power relations in modern society. In "The Subject and Power," Foucault had tried to clarify the stakes of his research from the very start: "I would like to say, first of all, what has been *the goal of my work during the last twenty years*. It has *not been to analyze the phenomena of power*, nor to elaborate the foundations of such an analysis. My objective, instead, has been to create a history of the different modes by which, in our culture, human beings are made subjects. *My work has dealt with three modes of subjectivation which transform human beings into subjects*" (Foucault 1982, 208, my emphasis).

Foucault's statements would seem unequivocal. Yet, the reconstruction of Foucault's thought offered by Dreyfus and Rabinow grants an absolutely central role to the analysis of power and, above all, of the concept of biopower.[14] This perspective informs their whole argument, their general narrative, the objections they advance, and the anticipation for future outcomes they expect from Foucault's journey. It is precisely from the repeated formulations of expectations that the sense of direct involvement experienced by the authors emerges most clearly. The following two passages from the beginning of chapter six, titled "From the Repressive Hypothesis to Biopower," show it well:

> In this section of our book, we lay out a synoptic overview of Foucault's general story, an account which, not surprisingly, follows the broad line of argumentation used here. We should

> stress that Foucault has never presented his work in quite this form. His work is still very much in a process of change and refinement. There are areas of unclearness and sketchiness which can be read either as confusion or, more sympathetically, as problems he has opened up for further exploration, either by his subsequent work or by others. (1982, 126)

> But as his interpretations gain more adherents and become — as they already have — stimuli to research, these problems will have to be thematized more explicitly or else they will all too likely be incorporated into empirical historical procedures. ([. . .] His silence does not help his cause. What may be an effective tactic in the intellectual field of Paris takes on a rather different function in the halls of American academia). (1982, 127)

Although they admit on several occasions that the work of Foucault, whose death two years later they could certainly not anticipate, may still hold upheavals and surprises,[15] they seem unwilling to acknowledge the sense of Foucault's clarifications about the position occupied by his research on power, or of the lines of research that the French philosopher had been following in those years. Even in the afterword, which appeared in the second edition of 1983, together with the long interview "On the Genealogy of Ethics: Compendium of a Work in Progress," Dreyfus and Rabinow do not relent:

> However, as we shall argue later, Foucault's focus on the technologies of the self *may have deflected concern* from what his work has singled out as the even greater and longer range dangers of Weberian rationalization, Heideggerian technology, and the normalization and destruction inherent in biopower. At this point, however, Foucault is devoting his attention to an area that, according to his diagnosis is more open to change, while bearing in mind that he will *eventually have to return* to a full-scale analysis of biopower. (1982, 254, my emphasis)

Dreyfus and Rabinow's interpretation has become a reference point for Foucauldian criticism.[16] Some of the interpretive guidelines it offered have also contributed to the generalized misunderstanding of the sense of the last part of Foucault's philosophical itinerary that I question in the following chapters[17] where I present my interpretation of Foucault's project and a discussion, at times explicit and at other times implicit, of Dreyfus and Rabinow's interpretation. In sum, Dreyfus and Rabinow suggest at least four interpretative theses that deserve to be rediscussed. First of all, they read Foucault's philosophical path fundamentally in terms of a methodological research. Second, and consequently, they claim that Foucault's itinerary can be essentially divided into two phases, whose transition was determined by an inversion of the hierarchy between theory and practice. Third, they single out the concept of biopower as the great contribution of Foucault's thought, and they see it as the *telos* that orients and gives meaning to the entire second phase of his philosophical journey. Finally, as mentioned in the previous section, their approach forces them to consider the final results of Foucault's studies as a turning point.[18] My reading of Foucault's path is centered on the elements of continuity, as well as on all the shifts and the apparently less significant adjustments, and it leverages a distance that is chronological as much as critical[19] although, as the cases of Schürmann and Deleuze suggest, the chronological proximity does not necessarily result in an incongruous interpretation. As Deleuze points out, "misunderstandings are often reactions of malicious stupidity. There are some who can only feel intelligent by discovering 'contradictions' in a great thinker" (1995, 90).

A Theoretical Framework

The expression *practical philosophy* is an explicit index to Aristotle's writings and to those authors who claimed their viability in the struggle against the perceived formalism and intellectualism of the pervasive Neo-Kantian ethics in the context of German debate on the so-called *Rehabilitirung der praktishen Philosophie* in the 1960s.[20] In Aristotle, the expression *practical philosophy* indicates the thought that deals with the ever singular, contingent, historically determined human actions. *Practical philosophy* has *praxis* both as its object and its task; it overcomes the distinction between ethics and politics by showing their necessary co-implication.

Here, I argue that the great novelty of Foucault's proposal consists of showing that practical thought is the only possible horizon of philosophy tout court. I use the expression *practical philosophy* to designate Foucault's conception of philosophy as such, including its object, its task, its methodology, and its limits. From this perspective, the expression does not refer to a specific philosophical discipline, but rather to a horizon of sense that allows us to gather and articulate all the different components of Foucault's thought. The expression allows us to grasp the deep non-systematic cohesion of a thought that is, at the same time, a philosophy of history, a political analysis, and an ethics. Throughout the book, I show how the concept of *practical philosophy* makes it possible to understand the profound consistency underlying Foucault's reflection and to validate his reiterated claim about the existence of a thematic and goal-oriented unity centered around the "issue of the subject."

Indeed, from the standpoint of *practical philosophy,* Foucault's overall philosophical itinerary appears as an effort to rethink philosophy, its categories, and its task that arises from the rejection of a metaphysics of the subject. Foucault carries out an *an-archaeo-genealogical* critique of the intersubjective and practically determined processes through which subjectivity is historically constituted. He structures his overall analysis of the subject around three axes corresponding to the subject's relation to truth, to others, and to themselves — the dimensions of knowledge, power, and ethics that represent his main concerns. Foucault is always addressing these three dimensions at the same time and from three different standpoints that we may identify as the deconstructive, constructive, and meta-philosophical perspectives. However, the three axes of Foucault's research trace a path that maps a single and unique territory — the single plane to which *practical philosophy* refers. It is *a plane of absolute immanence* because it is not *immanent to* anything — there is simply nothing that is not immanent to it (Deleuze 2001, 25–33). A thought striving to work this field is a *practical philosophy* because it is neither wholly historical, nor entirely philosophical. It must always keep "a double reference: to philosophy, which must be asked to explain how thought could have a history, and to history, which must be asked to produce the various forms of thought in whatever concrete forms they may assume (system of representations, institutions, practices)" (Foucault 1984, 336). Philosophical thinking must come to terms with how universality and generality unfold historically, as well as with its own historicity. Thought itself, understood as the form of human experience, that is, as the force forming and informing it, is inseparable from the practical dimension of the experience it shapes, and, therefore, it is always historically determined.

In this perspective, Foucault assigns to philosophy the critical task of questioning the present as a way of opening it to possible transformations. This is an essentially positive task that aims at delineating the specificity and contingence of the conditions defining the limits of individuals' autonomy with an eye to their possible overcoming. As critical task, *practical philosophy* must foreground the nonnecessity of the normative framework — Foucault's "regime of truth" — that determines the current historical form of individuals' relationship to truth as well as the forms of power relationships, and of individuals' relation to themselves. In other words, the "regime of truth" determines an individual's modes of subjectivation at a given moment. *Practical philosophy* seeks to emancipate the subjects from the regimes of truth in which they are entrapped, and to enable an active exercise of freedom, a possible transformation, and an autonomous subjectivation as a form of resistance. It strives to critically mediate the processes of subjectivation that allows the emancipation of single individuals and groups from the heteronomous modes of subjectivation. The heteronomous modes of subjectivation include both the exterior modes producing objectivation into knowledge formation and the related forms of domination through institutional power relationships, as well as the internalized modes generating identitarian individuation.[21] The critical mediating task that binds Foucault's *practical philosophy* to the present is certainly political, and yet it has always already also ethical and epistemological dimensions.

Practical philosophy names Foucault's suggested overcoming of the philosophy of the subject through the *an-archaeo-genealogy* of its historical constitution in different normative contexts. It is a positive project that recasts freedom as the possibility to produce autonomous forms of subjectivation, and it is inseparable from the task to recast philosophy's goal as critical and emancipatory. The horizon of *practical philosophy* encompasses the critical-deconstructive,

constructive, and meta-philosophical instances that jointly determine how Foucault deals with the issue of the subject. We can understand the sense in which Foucault considers the issue of the subject as the "goal" and the "general theme" of his research only if we focus on these three instances.

Foucault's *practical philosophy*, so conceived, is marked by a sui generis principle that — adopting the expression Reiner Schürmann coined for his major work on Heidegger's thought — I call *the principle of anarchy*. My borrowing is meant to stress how, for Foucault, the lack of a metaphysical universal and abstract foundational ground — in other words, the lack of an *arché* — turns into a productive principle. The missing *arché* does not end up in a nihilistic denial. On the contrary, it becomes the engine of the deconstructive work focused on the opening of a positive space of freedom. It is a freedom understood as the active production of a subjectivity that is *auto-nomous* with respect to the normative framework and *an-archic* insofar as it is not determined by the *arché* that constitutes the subject's identity as the internalized form of the currently prevailing regime of truth. The principle of anarchy concerns the practice of a *practical philosophy* whose goal is to suggest — at a specific moment — a possible discontinuity from the norm as the principle ruling the organization of the real world. The principle must not be translated into the political ambition to avoid government. From a political standpoint, Foucault's principle of anarchy produces instead a relative an-archism that questions the specific normative framework — not the norm as such, as much as any particular norm. On the other hand, the principle of anarchy prevents the transformation of the critical work the practical philosopher carries out into a prescriptive or a normative principle. The critical work can only produce the contingent practice of a philosophical virtue, or an *ēthos*, as Foucault explained, via the patient study of the Greek concept of *parrhēsia* he conducted in his last three years of teaching at the *Collège de France*.

Finally, Foucault's *practical philosophy* may run into two kinds of problems, which Foucault himself seems to have recognized although not solved. The first problem concerns the always contingent *philosophical heroism* that the practice of freedom seems to require, because the critical mediation of the processes of subjectivation depends upon the instauration of a specific philosophical *ēthos* that would "bring to light transformable singularities" (1984, 335). Second, the necessary philosophical mediation of all subjectivation processes runs the risk of replacing the institutionalized heteronomy of the current regime of truth with the charismatic heteronomy of the philosopher. This way the philosopher's influence may introduce a new form of subalternity by turning an alterity that was meant to be emancipatory into a subjectivizing force. There is a risk of a philosophical aristocracy, a true *philoso-cracy*.

Outline

Michel Foucault's Practical Philosophy is organized into four chapters. The first chapter introduces the concept of *practical philosophy* as the interpretive framework of Foucault's thought and presents an overall reading of his work on such a basis. In the last three chapters, the book offers a diachronic consideration of Foucault's itinerary from the introduction of the relational paradigm of power in the 1970s to the last courses at the *Collège de France* in the 1980s. The choice to limit the diachronic consideration to this ten-year time frame has to do with the goal of questioning the common claim of a "radical turn" in Foucault's work, leading him to abandon the political dimension of thought to retreat into the ethical sphere. In chapters 2 to 4, the interpretation of Foucault's thought as *practical philosophy* is put to the test by showing how such an interpretation allows us to better understand the internal logic and the inner reasons that led Foucault through his various conceptual shifts. Chapters 2 and 3 discuss the Foucauldian analysis of power/knowledge relationships (2) and trace the crisis that prompted him to replace the power/knowledge pair with the idea of a "government of men by the truth" (3), showing the role that the analysis played by the Christian model of pastoral power in such a shift. This conceptual reorientation is key to question the traditional aforementioned interpretation that focuses on an "ethical turn." The concept of "government of truth" allows Foucault to reorganize into a single framework the interweaving of connections that link together what he considers the three main axes of every experience: "the forms of a possible knowledge," "the normative matrices of individual behavior," and finally, "the virtual modes of existence of possible subjects." It clears the path for a transition from the questioning of subjugation processes to an investigation of the possibilities of individual autonomous subjectivation. This transition, rather than a "turning point" in the direction of an ethical retreat, or of a return to the subject, represents a further step toward a radicalization of Foucault's thought in the direction of a *practical philosophy* that is seeking the possibility of thinking *freedom* in the strongest possible sense. The last chapter examines the analyses of *parrhēsia* and *critique* that Foucault dealt with in his last few courses. I show how the questions about the possibility of individuals playing an active role in the processes of subjectivation, about freedom as the autonomous and anarchic production of one's own subjectivity, and about philosophy's task as critical mediation emerges naturally from the concept of "government of men by the truth," thereby bringing the hermeneutic circle this work proposes to its closure. Finally, the afterword addresses directly the question of the legacy of Foucault's *practical philosophy*.

1
Practical Philosophy as the Horizon of Foucault's Thought

I think subjectivation has little to do with any subject. It's to do, rather, with an electric or magnetic field, an individuation taking place through intensities (weak as well as strong ones), it's to do with individuated fields, not persons or identities. It's what Foucault, elsewhere, calls "passion." This idea of subjectivation in Foucault is no less original than those of power and knowledge: the three together constitute a way of living, *a strange three-dimensional figure*, as well as the greatest of modern philosophies (and I say this without joking).

— Deleuze 1995, my emphasis

What is the philosophical horizon of Foucault's path, with all its displacements, adjustments, and occasional deviations? Paraphrasing Deleuze, the question is: what is the *whole* of Foucault's thought, the inner *logic* that forces him to move from one level to the next, from one *crisis* to the next? Deleuze's answer is that such a logic is a *strange three-dimensional figure* organized by *knowledge*, *power*, and *subjectivation*. Accepting Deleuze's suggestion and developing it further, I maintain that such a whole whose inner logic ties together the different dimensions of Foucault's thought is that of a *practical philosophy*. This means that the idea of *practical philosophy* represents Foucault's specific philosophical horizon and it, therefore, also provides the appropriate framework to understand his intellectual path.

On several occasions, Foucault insisted that the issue of the subject had always been the overall central theme of his research. The already quoted passage from the first section — titled, not by chance, "Why Study Power: the Issue of the Subject" — of "Subject and Power," provides ample confirmation: "I would like to say, first of all, what has been the goal of my work during the last twenty years. It has not been to analyze the phenomena of power, nor to elaborate the foundations of such an analysis. My objective, instead, has been *to create a history of the different modes by which, in our culture, human beings are made subjects*" (Foucault 1982, 208, my emphasis).

Understanding how Foucault's retrospective gaze came to single out the issue of the subject as the overarching principle that allowed him to draw a critical assessment of his analyses is the starting point of this book. What is at stake is establishing how exactly and to what extent such an issue determines the specificity of Foucault's thought. On the one hand, the problem of subjectivity provides the core of the critical context from which the perspective of Foucault's *practical philosophy* emerges. On the other hand, the concept of *subjectivation* plays a key role in the general configuration of Foucault's project, in particular with respect to the joint concepts of archaeology and genealogy. It is indeed starting from the gap separating subjectivity and subjectivation that one can begin to understand the boundaries and implications of *practical philosophy* considered as the horizon of sense of Foucault's philosophical itinerary. Since the concept of *practical philosophy* is both the product as well as the prerequisite of the interpretive process, the full philosophical import of such implications only appears at the end of the book — once the hermeneutic circle, which always binds the object under scrutiny to its meaning through the interpretation, has been fully traced. The discussion of the most important aspects of the massive secondary literature on Foucault's thought from the previous chapter continues alongside the whole process. In particular, it is important to engage with the four hermeneutic axes that Dreyfus and Rabinow have advanced in their monograph: the methodological interpretation of Foucault's path and its articulation in two phases marked by the inversion of the theory/practice relationship; the concept of biopower as the climax and *telos* of his philosophical path; and finally, the reading of Foucault's late research as a *turn*.

The Critique of Subjectivism

The problem of subjectivity is a key critical focal point allowing Foucault's overall project to take shape. The critique of the philosophical category of the subject appears very early in his thought, and he will never abandon it. It is the leading thread guiding him when he distances himself from phenomenology and Marxism and, more generally, when he defines himself against the contemporary philosophical landscape (particularly, against structuralism).[1] Furthermore, Foucault's effort to bring subjectivity back onto historical terrain — a task that continues Nietzsche's historicization of the subject, as he acknowledges[2] — starts from a critique of the grounds of modern philosophy and the foundational priority it assigns to the subject-substance, as well as from a rejection of all forms of universalism, humanism, and the sense-giving Husserlian subject.[3] Generally speaking, Foucault does not organize his *exit from the philosophy of the subject* systematically: the Foucauldian genealogy of the modern subject does not present itself as a series of precise analyses following the path that leads from Descartes to Sartre. On each occasion, Foucault deals with the different thinkers as expressions of a philosophy of the subject that must be questioned and kept at a distance. When he discusses Descartes, Kant, or Husserl, what matters to Foucault is the milestone role these authors play in the genealogical reconstruction he is providing. It is in this sense that he looks critically at Descartes as the founder of the subject of modern science, as well as to phenomenology and existentialism:

> What I rejected was the idea of starting out with a theory of the subject — as is done, for example, in phenomenology or existentialism — and, on the basis of this theory, asking how a given form of knowledge was possible. What I wanted to try to show was how the subject constituted itself, in one specific form or another, as a mad or a healthy subject, as a delinquent or non-delinquent subject, through certain practices that were also game of truth, practices of power, etc. (Foucault 1996, 440)

In a brief aside opening up one of his 1980s American lectures, Foucault stated that the philosophy of the subject — which enjoyed a dominant role in France before WWII already, partly due to French academia's traditional subjection to Descartes and partly due to Husserl's influence — received a further impulse as a result of the emotional shock caused by the experiences of massacres and authoritarianism. It is only at the end of this historical phase that the central role of the subject begins to vacillate and is questioned from multiple philosophical perspectives. Foucault is well aware that he shares the same critical attitude with analytic philosophy and structuralism, yet he never tires of underlining the specificity of his approach:

> With the all too easy clarity of hindsight — what you call, I think, the "Monday morning quarterback" — let me say that there were two possible paths that led beyond this philosophy of the subject. First, the theory of objective knowledge and, two, an analysis of systems of meaning, or semiology. The first of these was the path of logical positivism. The second was that of a certain school of linguistics, psychoanalysis, and anthropology, all generally grouped under the rubric of structuralism. These were not the directions I took. [. . .] I have tried to get out from the philosophy of the subject through a genealogy of the subject, by studying the constitution of the subject across history which had led us to the modern concept of the self. This has not always been an easy task, since most of historians prefer a history of social processes, and most philosophers prefer a subject without history. (Foucault 2016a, 22)

Foucault rejects all ahistorical conceptions of an a priori, always already given, self-identical subject that would provide an indisputable epistemological foundation as well as an abstract and universal normative morality. He rejects humanism as the approach that leverages a unique, transhistorical, and universal *human nature* expressing the truth of man and traces it in the most disparate philosophical contexts, from Christianity to Marxism, from national socialism to existentialism. Indeed, this kind of humanism is the "network that links thoughts of the positivist or eschatological type (Marxism being in the first rank of these) and reflections inspired by phenomenology" (Foucault 1970, 321).

In *The Order of Things*, the critique of humanism takes the shape of an archaeological reconstruction of the birth of the so-called human sciences. Foucault emphasizes the substantial difference between the classic epistemology embodied in Cartesian thought and the new paradigm that Kant inaugurated, and that he labels the "analytics of finitude." In the classic model, the subject's representation of things is direct, positive, and problem free. In the Kantian model, on the other hand, the appearance of an allotropy between empirical data and transcendental schemata will eventually enable the formation of the human sciences whose archaeology Foucault is reconstructing. "For the threshold of our modernity is situated not by the attempt to apply objective methods to the study of man, but rather by the constitution of an empirico-transcendental doublet which was called *man*" (Foucault 1970, 319, emphasis in original).

The critique of the philosophy of the subject was the ground for Foucault's distancing from Marxism, which he considered a failed attempt to overcome metaphysics.[4] Foucault's objections[5] are mostly aimed at the dogmatism of a widely accepted Marxist popularization rather than at Marx's thought.[6] Though sparse and fragmented,[7] Foucault's critique of Marxism exhibits a certain constancy and continuity:

> It goes without saying — and it goes even better if we say it — that neither materialism nor the theory of ideologies successfully constituted a theory of objectivity or of signification. Marxism put itself forward as a humanistic discourse that could replace the abstract subject with an appeal to the real man, to the concrete man. It should have been clear at the time that Marxism carried with it a fundamental theoretical and practical weakness: the humanistic discourse hid the political reality that the Marxists of this period nonetheless supported. (Foucault 2016a, 21–22)

From Foucault's perspective, the Marxist interpretation of reality on the basis of *human nature* or of the *laws* of historical development is still humanistic. Its attempted overcoming of the subject's abstract character through a foregrounding of the human beings' material condition of existence is still vitiated by the anthropologism, universalism, and essentialism of a modern *episteme* always concealing the processes of subjectivation's historicity.[8]

Furthermore, Foucault detects an implicit reference to a subject and its virtual opposition to an absolute truth in the concept of ideology, as well as the reference to a series of dualistic structure oppositions like true/false, scientific/unscientific, reality/appearance, and rational/irrational that are characteristic of modern subjectivism and representational systems.⁹

Foucault's critique of Marxism goes beyond the super-structural level and directly targets the *economist* principle underlying the Marxist conception of class relationships at the deeper structural level.¹⁰ Foucault considers Marxism a totalizing theoretical model that adopts economics as the universal, all-encompassing principle that grounds all domination dynamics and provides political power with its very raison d'être. Finally, Foucault's critique of the subjectivism that some versions of Marxism entail is directed also at their theory of power, because he considers them unable to overcome a substantially ontological conception that remains prisoner of the classical theory of sovereignty.¹¹ Both the firmly established central role of the state apparatus and the wholeness of power show that Marxism runs into the same limitations of the classical, rights-based political theory. In spite of its emphasis on the state as the target of social struggles and its insistence on the repressive function of power, Marxism produces the same effects: it conceals the strategic mechanisms of power relationships and socio-political reality. The next chapter, devoted precisely to a discussion of the issue of power, provides a more extensive discussion of the latter critiques.¹²

The "systematic skepticism toward all anthropological universals" guiding all Foucault's investigations comes from the critical perspective that I just outlined (Foucault 2003c, 3). As he wrote in the pages devoted to him in the *Dictionnaire des philosophes*,

> The first rule of method for this kind of work is this: insofar as possible, circumvent the anthropological universals (and, of course, those of a humanism that would assert the rights, the privileges, and the nature of a human being as an immediate and timeless truth of the subject), *in order to examine them as historical constructs*. One must also *reverse the philosophical way of proceeding upward to the constituent subject* which is asked to account for every possible object of knowledge in general [. . .] *refusing the philosophical recourse to a constituent subject* does not mean to acting as if the subject did not exist, making an abstraction of it on behalf of a pure objectivity. (Foucault 2003c, 3, my emphasis)

The systematic skepticism Foucault invokes is a consequence of what I later call, borrowing Reiner Schürmann's expression, *the principle of anarchy*; this is what provides the starting point of his *practical philosophy* project.¹³ The Foucauldian analyses that *interrogate the historicity* and highlight the contingency of all the categories and all universal and necessary principles based on the essential truth of a transhistorical subject — their chronological and thematic heterogeneity notwithstanding — are also based on his systematic skepticism. To question the essential historicity of anthropological universals means to question both the historicity of their foundation and the historicity of the subject. In other words, "reversing the philosophical way of proceeding upward to the constituent subject" means to examine how the subject constitutes itself historically through "games of truth" in which individuals function both as subjects as well as objects of knowledge; through strategic relationships of power; and through specific modes of self-relationship.[14]

These three modes of the subjectivation process — modes that, as I show below, are first and foremost practical — are the three axes, corresponding to an equal number of phases, around which Foucault retrospectively organizes his research. Through the years, Foucault always follows this threefold partition, even though he changes the phrasing to emphasize its complex structure of cross-references and mutual entailment as much as possible.

The Analysis of Subjectivation Processes via Archaeology and Genealogy

According to Foucault, examining the historical constitution of the subject does not mean placing a universal subject within historical processes, historicizing its relationship to truth, or relativizing its representations and interpretations.

> I don't believe that the problem can be solved by historicizing the subject as posited by the phenomenologists, fabricating a subject that evolves through the course of history. One has to dispense with the constituent subject, to get rid of the subject itself, that's to say, to arrive at an analysis that can account for the constitution of the subject within a historical framework. And this is what I would call genealogy, that is a form of history that can account for the constitution of the knowledges, discourses, domains of objects, and so on, without having to make reference to a subject that is either transcendental in relation to the field of events or runs in its empty sameness throughout the course of history. (Foucault 1984, 59)

The processes by which individuals self-constitute and recognize themselves as subjects must be considered historical. "Reversing the philosophical way of proceeding upward to the constituent subject" (Foucault 2003c, 3) requires a historical analysis of the processes of subjectivation.

A proper grasp of the concept of *subjectivation* allows us to understand both the logic underlying the crises and displacements of Foucault's thought and in which general sense he could integrate three different phases of his work into a unified coherent philosophical project. From the perspective of subjectivation processes, one can understand the relationship between the so-called archaeological and genealogical phases of Foucault's thought in terms of continuity.

As mentioned above, Foucault identifies three types of processes of this kind. There are processes concerning the subject-object relationship as knowledge is formed; processes concerning power relationships between subjects; finally, processes concerning the subject's relationship to itself.

During the process of knowledge formation, the individual constitutes itself as a subject of knowledge in relationship to something given as object within the same relationship. As the relationship comes into being, the subject is subjectivized and the object objectivized, thereby producing what Foucault calls "games of truth" — sets of rules governing the production of truth and the articulation of discourses responding to criteria of truth or falsity. Foucault is particularly interested in the games of truth producing a form of knowledge in which the subject becomes its own object — in other words, the so-called human sciences as theories of the speaking, living, and acting subject. During the 1960s, Foucault focuses on questioning these processes on the exclusively discursive level through the practice of archaeology, in which "it's precisely a matter of recapturing the construction of a *connaissance* — that is, of a relation between a fixed subject and a domain of objects, in his historical roots, in this movement of *savoir* which makes the construction possible" (Foucault 2001a, 256, emphasis in original).

With the archaeology of knowledge, Foucault seeks the *historical a-priori* that allowed the production of a determined discursive event — the game of truth that, on each occasion, turned a specific object into an object of knowledge. He is interested in the historical formation of an allegedly absolute *episteme*. The archaeological approach reconsiders from the standpoint of their historical contingency, those particular statements, introduced as universal atemporal truths, in which individuals are supposed to recognize themselves.

Foucault's *archaeology* does not refer to the methodology archaeologists use — or at least not only to that. He mostly uses it because of its implicit references to both the *arché* and the archive.[15]

The *arché*, understood as foundational principle, interests Foucault because it represents the opposite of his philosophical outlook. Foucault himself alluded to it when he jokingly introduced the term *anarchaeology* in the 1980 course at the *Collège de France*. Foucault deploys the pun — with a wink to the debates about his alleged anarchism — to highlight the peculiarity of his approach against all analyses based on ideology. His own "systematic skepticism toward all anthropological universals" — the principle of anarchy introduced in the previous section — lies in stark contrast to the concealed humanist and universalist perspective of ideology critique. Foucauldian analyses never attempt to explain a given phenomenon on the basis of a universal principle or an essential characteristic of human nature. On the contrary, they always seek to assess the historical specificity of all phenomena based on the particular contingency in which they are immersed.

The reference to the archive is important to properly grasp Foucault's later shift from archaeology to genealogy — a shift that is more consistent with his own understanding of methodology. Contrary to Dreyfus and Rabinow's critical suggestion, I do not think we can read Foucault's path as methodological research. There is methodological research, but it is fully immanent to the investigation's own development. The conceptual tools and the analytical setup Foucault deploys are continuously evolving, yet this evolution is determined by the emerging needs of his research. On this point, Foucault is crystal clear:

> I do not have a method that I would apply in the same way to different domains. On the contrary, I would say that there is a fixed domain of objects which I have tried to isolate using instruments that I find or forge at the very same time as I am doing my research without privileging the problem of method. [. . .] I have tried to correct my instruments beginning with the objects I believe I found, and at this time the correct instrument shows me that the object I defined is not that: thus I waver and hesitate from book to book. (Foucault 1994a, nn. 216, 404–05)

The archive is not understood as a mere witness to the past, but as an open dimension in the present's historical space that shows its intrinsic ties to past discursive events.[16] As Judith Revel aptly remarked, the emphasis on the connection with the present shows the continuity between the archaeological and genealogical analyses, even though the link is more directly and vertically played out in the latter (Revel 2003, 68). Thus, there is no forsaking the archaeological method in favor of genealogy, nor a radical methodological change prompted by the inversion of the theory/practice and discourses/practices hierarchies. Rather, the investigation redoubles as a consequence of the greater complexity of the conceptual framework Foucault traces.

In the 1971 essay "Nietzsche, Genealogy, History," genealogy opposes the search for an origin that would provide the kernel of an essential primordial truth preceding all that is exterior and accidental. Genealogy opposes any metaphysical interpretation of history positing as origin an ideal teleological destination, including Marxism's materialistic teleology. It rather aims at the uniqueness of the events as it retrieves our provenance from the dispersal of accidents and from the radical exteriority of events and their intrinsic contingency. Our provenance is gained from a history kept in its actual discontinuity. When Foucault insists on the central role of the event, he distances himself from structuralism's systematic effort to remove contingency from science. However, advancing contingency within a genealogical framework means also "to avoid trying to do for the event what was previously done with the concept of structure [. . .] to distinguish among events, to differentiate the networks and levels to which they belong, and to reconstitute the lines along which they are connected and engender one another" (Foucault 2001d, 116). Foregrounding contingency means that although historical events lack a *dialectical* meaning or a specific structure, they are not thereby considered incoherent, unintelligible, or random.

It is not until the 1970s that Foucault managed to single out power as the central problem to investigate. The interrogation of power comes into play to explain the discontinuities and the transformations occurring in the rules governing the formation of scientific discourses that can be accepted as true. In a 1976 interview, Foucault — while not hiding some disappointment for the difficulties he encountered — concedes that *The Order of Things* and *The History of Madness* were lacking an explicit discussion of discursive or truth regimens (Foucault 2001d, 113–15). Both works were lacking a discussion of the effects of power specific to scientific discourse. Truth is not an otherworldly entity waiting to be discovered by some superior intellect, nor a hidden meaning to be ascertained. Truth is neither pure nor universal but historical: it is produced, diffused, and sustained on the basis of the power relationships that cross it and in view of the power effects it generates. Each truth, in other words, is tied to the specific regime of truth that a determinate society enforces at a given time. Such a regime of truth is not to equate with ideology because it is not a superstructural phenomenon, but it rather represents the set of historical conditions presiding over the formation and the operation of every economic, political, and social system, for it determines all discursive practices and intersubjective relationships. As Daniele Lorenzini in *The Force of Truth* clearly shows, this does not mean that truth is reducible to power or that Foucault would be a relativist. Rather — as it became clear in the 1980s — while truth established autonomously according to the set of rules each game of truth defines, those rules as well as the acceptance and enforcement of the practical implications of truth depend on the specific regime of truth to which the game belongs.[17]

It becomes apparent that the epistemological aspect of the processes of subjectivation cannot be kept separate from the power networks within which individuals are always operating. Thus, genealogy intervenes alongside archaeology to better account for the subjectivation of individuals as subjects and objects of knowledge. "Three domains of genealogy are possible. First, a historical ontology of ourselves in relation to truth through which we constitute ourselves as subjects of knowledge; second, a historical ontology of ourselves in relation to a field of power through which we constitute ourselves as subjects acting on others; third, a historical ontology of ourselves in relation to ethics through which we constitute ourselves as moral agents" (Foucault 1997c, 262). The relationship of the individual with itself corresponds then to a third dimension of experience through which another kind of subjectivation process takes place. What Foucault calls "technologies of the self" are concerned with this relationship of the individual with itself. These are techniques that individuals may use to transform themselves and actively constitute themselves as subject through a positive experience of freedom. As we see below, Foucault devoted his entire work of the 1980s to the study of these *ethical-poietic* techniques and to the relationships of mutual implication with the other modes of subjectivation.

It is far from obvious how to carry out the transition from the *an-archaeo-genealogical* analysis of the processes of subjectivation in the field of power relationships to the investigation of the modes of autonomous self-constitution that the individual may pursue through specific instances of self-relationship. The elucidation of this transition is one of the main critical knots that this book wishes to untie. As I mentioned, several interpreters see it as a *turn* resulting from a break and a decisive change of direction from Foucault's previous itinerary. Instead, what is at stake in my analysis is to show how, thanks to the idea of *practical philosophy*, it becomes possible to understand *the logic* that led *Foucault's thought* through this transition and to grasp its coherence through at least two important displacements. The task ahead requires us to follow the development of Foucault's analyses of knowledge-power relationships (chapter 2) and to trace the genesis of the crisis that produced the need to replace power/knowledge with the concept of "government of men by the truth" (chapter 3). Only then, it becomes clear how the latter concept compelled Foucault to examine the possibility that individuals may freely and actively take part in the processes of subjectivation he had previously deemed fully heteronomous (chapter 4).

Knowledge, power, and technologies of the self are the three issues or, as Foucault calls them during the 1983 course, the three mutually articulating and reciprocally illuminating "focuses of experience," that follow each other throughout his philosophical itinerary.

> I tried to mark out three types of problems: that of truth, that of power, and that of individual conduct. These three domains of experience can be understood only in relation to each other and only with each other. What hampered me in the preceding books was to have considered the first two experiences without taking into account the third. By bringing this last experience to light, I had a guiding thread which didn't need to be justified by resorting to rhetorical methods by which one could avoid one of the three fundamental domains of experience. (Foucault 1996, 466)

The newly introduced discussion of individual ethical possibilities — or of *the care of the self as a practice of freedom,* to quote the title of a well-known 1984 interview — leads Foucault to a retrospective reconstruction of the leading thread that guided him down his research path. It may have been a self-reflection on his own *ēthos* as a philosopher that prompted the new emphasis, or perhaps it was a need to assess philosophical practice as an exercise of freedom and its possible effects on socio-political reality. However, we need to point out the illegitimacy of reading this phase of Foucault's work as an ethical turn that would have followed his initially prevailing theoretical interest and the subsequent political focus.

It is true that these "techniques of the self" become an essential component of Foucault's reflection on the possibility of autonomy within subjectivation processes. Yet they emerge in the context of the analysis of heteronomous modes of subjectivation. At first, Foucault examines how the coercion- and subjection-oriented government of others resorts to processes in which the individual acts upon itself. He considers how government of self could be an instrument of heteronomous subjectivation. It is only in a second moment, in particular through his extended confrontation with classical ethics, that Foucault interrogates the possibility of an active exercise of freedom directly within subjectivation processes, and he raises the issue of ethics as its autonomous practical exercise.[18] At this point, the explicit and urgent questioning of the task of philosophy becomes imperative for a thought that puts itself forth as *practical philosophy*. This questioning offers Foucault a chance for critical self-assessment focused on the role that a philosopher may assume in subjectivation processes. He then elicits the question about its possible emancipatory role, its conditions, and its limitations within the constraints of heteronomous subjectivation processes. Foucault's analysis of the Greek concept of *parrhēsia*,[19] which kept him busy for three academic years, and his reiterated confrontations with Kant over the *Aufklärung* and on critique as philosophical *ēthos* must be placed in this context.[20]

Foucault's Practical Philosophy and the Principle of Anarchy

Practical philosophy is the horizon of understanding of Foucault's thought. This statement implies that the horizon singled out by the expression *practical philosophy* is the main reference for the understanding of Foucault's critical standpoint, his goals, and his whole developmental path. It also implies that such a horizon gives us a handle on how Foucault relates the particular task he assigns to his own thought to the task of philosophy in general.

By taking seriously Foucault's statement about the subject as his main theme, one can see that the questioning of the modern subject as the abstract, universal, foundational ground is the critical starting point of the Foucauldian project. It follows that all allegedly universal and necessity-bound anthropological and political models — the poisoned fruits of a subjectivist-humanist philosophical standpoint — must also be questioned. From this critical perspective one can understand the principle of anarchy that underwrites the suggestion of a *practical philosophy*.

I borrow the expression *principle of anarchy* from Reiner Schürmann's monograph on Heidegger (1984), not only because I find it particularly fitting, but also because Schürmann's essay on Foucault (1986) is an essential critical referent of my reading. Moreover, the expression *principle of anarchy* — whose obvious paradox skirts the oxymoron — somehow resonates, both in style and intent, with a number of concepts Foucault uses to explain the specificity of his perspective. I am referring, for instance, to the concepts of *historical a-priori*, *historical ontology*, not to mention the playful joke about the term *an-archaeology* that Foucault used in the 1980 lecture I discussed in the previous section. The meanings of all these expressions, and of the principle of anarchy as well, leverage paradox to bring forth the tension between the critical-deconstructive and the similarly strong analytic-constructive components of Foucault's project. I turn to the principle of anarchy to emphasize that Foucault's rejection of the *arché* does not end in a negative philosophical perspective, nor in a nihilistic stance. On the contrary, it becomes the principle for a *positive* philosophy that constitutes itself as a *practical philosophy*. Foucault opposes his *an-archaeo-genealogy* to the onto-theology of subjectivist-humanist philosophy.

What underwrites Foucault's proposal is the idea that philosophy must be torn away both from the metaphysical model of the *arché* and from the reference to foundational ground that functions both as origin and meaning-donating *telos*. It is the idea contained in the rejection of "a philosophical recourse to a constituent subject" (Foucault 2003c, 3) and in the adoption of a "systematic skepticism towards all anthropological universals" (Foucault 2003c, 3). The achievement of such a skeptical rejection is not an abandonment, but rather a reversal of the given perspective and a reframing of the philosophical categories from an *an-archical* standpoint. Philosophy is reconfigured as a *practical philosophy* that turns the universality, abstractness, trans-historicity, and necessity of the *arché* into the singularity, concreteness, historicity, and contingency of the event. Foucault's *practical philosophy* is an alternative answer to the dilemma between "philosophical anthropology and social history," an answer such that it compels us "to think the very historicity of the forms of experience" (Foucault 1984, 334).

Foucault's philosophy is practical, not because it deals with "practical" issues, nor because it is a philosophical subfield separate from "theoretical" philosophy. It is not *practical* as the result of Foucault's alleged decision — at a specific moment of his thought's development — to reverse the hierarchy of theory and practice in favor of the latter, as Dreyfus and Rabinow's reading would have it.[21] And finally, Foucault's *practical philosophy* is not even advocated as a polemical move meant to return epistemological primacy to practical knowledge thereby lending legitimacy to the philosophical investigation of human praxis, as was the case with *Rehabilitierung der praktischen Philosophie*, which re-proposed Aristotle's *practical philosophy*, at the beginning of the 1960s, over and against the intellectualism and theoreticism of modern thought.[22]

Foucault's philosophy is *practical* tout court because the principle of anarchy undermines the distinction between theory and practice. The horizon of praxis becomes a "plane of immanence" where the *an-archaeo-genealogical* critique of the limits and the historico-practical conditioning of the processes of subjectivation takes place. Inquiring into the possibility of emancipatory and autonomous subjectivation processes, such a critique replaces the critique of the transcendental conditions of possibility of a given subject's epistemologically oriented experience. "Immanence is not related to *Some Thing* as a unity superior to all things or to a Subject as an act that brings about a synthesis of things: it is only when immanence is no longer immanence to anything other than itself that we can speak of a plane of immanence. No more than the transcendental field is defined by consciousness can the plane of immanence be defined by a subject or an object that is able to contain it" (Deleuze 2001, 27).

The practical plane of immanence is a single plane, but it is not smooth: it is discontinuous and made up of events and singularities whose contingency defines its conditions as well as its possible transformations — it presents what has happened and has been thought already as well as the virtual future that may be made and thought. Aristotle's *practical philosophy* dealt with the possible and the contingent, which meant it dealt with the part of reality that could be changed. For Foucault, accordingly, the whole spectrum of the real and the virtual falls within the scope of *practical philosophy* if we take practical to designate — as Aristotle did — everything connected to the present and to the fragility of the *now*, everything that could also not have been or that could have been otherwise. Since the practical refers to all that is singular, contingent, and historically and intersubjectively determined, it follows that, under the principle of anarchy, everything is practical. Under the principle of anarchy, thought can no longer choose to address the field of universal and necessary truths because there are no atemporal truths, first principles, and transcendental categories; yet thought cannot simply negate them — it must rethink them on the basis of their practical and historically determined conditions. At the same time, thought cannot represent itself as separate from action and as free from contingent conditions to the extent that thought represents *the very form of action*.

Thus, Foucault's philosophy is practical in a twofold sense: it conceives itself as a form of action and as the exercise of historically determined freedom and it holds a practical conception of the objects of such an exercise because nothing lying outside experience can ever be given. As the original (and later discarded) introduction *The Use of Pleasure* shows, the two aspects are indissolubly linked. There, Foucault presented the guidelines of his philosophical project as follows:

> There is no experience which is not a way of thinking, and which cannot be analyzed from the point of view of the history of thought; this is what might be called the principle of irreducibility of thought. According to a second principle, *this thought has a historicity which is proper to it. That it should have this historicity does not mean it is deprived of all universal form, but instead that putting into play of these universal forms is itself historical.* And that this historicity should be proper to it does not mean that it is independent of all the other historical

> determinations (of an economic, social, or political order), but that it has complex relations with them which always leave their specificity to the forms, transformations, and events of thought. This is what could be called the principle of singularity of the history of thought: there are events of thought. (Foucault 1997a, 201, my emphasis)

The idea of *practical philosophy* offers us the horizon of understanding we need to better grasp that *strange three-dimensional figure*, which, according to Deleuze, defines Foucault's thought as a *whole*. The *reversal of the appeal to the constituent subject* that Foucault invokes happens along three synchronic dimensions: the *an*-archaeology of knowledge, the *an-archaeo-genealogy* of the modes of subjectivation and the related techniques at work in all power relationships, and lastly the critique of the modalities of autonomous subjectivation. The Foucauldian answer to the problem of subjectivity starts from the *practical* standpoint and takes shape along these three dimensions. "Reversing the appeal to the constituent subject" (Foucault 2003c, 3) means, according to Foucault, thinking of a subjectivity that constitutes itself historically and *practically*. It constitutes itself at a specific time and within a determined normative and relational context, both as the object of power techniques and as the subject of ascetic practices pursued through punctual, contingent, discontinuous, discursive, and non-discursive events. Foucault holds that subjectivity must be rethought as practical because thought is inseparable from action. Thought is acting and, as such, it is always historically and intersubjectively determined. All human beings are living and thinking beings, and their thinking and acting cannot be separated: experience can only be given in the interrelation between action and thought. Foucault maintains that the separation between social history and the history of ideas is simply meaningless.[23] "By 'thought,' I mean what establishes, in a variety of possible forms, the play of true and false, and consequently constitutes the human being as a knowing subject [*sujet de connaissance*]; in other words, it is the basis for accepting or refusing rules, and constitutes human beings as social and juridical subjects; it is what establishes the relation with oneself and with others, and constitutes the human being as ethical subject" (Foucault 1997a, 200). Ethics, politics, and knowledge are the three possible domains of action of the practical subject, as well as the three domains to which thought refers in order to accompany and shape its actions. They are the three possible forms of experience whereby individuals constitute themselves as subjects. *Practical philosophy*'s investigation of the historical constitution of subjectivity is completely orthogonal to the traditional disciplinary subdivisions of philosophy. There is only one practical subjectivity and the "study of forms of experience can thus proceed from an analysis of 'practices' — discursive or not — as long as one qualifies that word to mean the different systems of action insofar as they are inhabited by thought as I have characterized it here" (Foucault 1997a, 201).

The main goal of *practical philosophy* is not *eupraktein* — the search for good and socially beneficial actions as the exercise of a practical wisdom [*phronesis*] aimed at the realization of the concrete human happiness instantiating its universal nature [*eudaimonia*]. Foucault's goal is to "consider the very historicity of forms of experience" (Foucault 1997a, 200) while also aiming at their possible transformation. Foucault's *practical philosophy* does not interrogate human action to assess its means toward an end, nor does it question duty as the transcendental ground of moral behavior. It assesses the possibility of freedom within historically given constraints. Its purview entails both a reframing of the concept of human freedom, including the possibility of resistance and emancipation, as well as a redefinition of philosophy's tasks.

The most important goal of Foucault's *practical philosophy*'s is to open a space of positive, *ēthos-poietic* freedom understood as the possibility that individuals have to operate creatively on their subjectivity. This freedom is not the abstract attribute of a universal substance, regardless of whether that attribute is conceived as the fundamental characteristic of the *truly human* nature or as the necessary prerequisite of any juridical-political theory. This freedom is fundamentally practical because it concerns the real and concrete possibilities individuals may have as they constitute themselves as autonomous subjects, even though the existing normative frameworks and the regimes of truth in which they operate are always predetermining those very same possibilities.

According to Foucault, freedom is the necessary precondition for the establishment of power relationships, and it represents the possibility of resisting technologies of subjugation and emancipating oneself from heteronomous subjectivation. The power relationships that produce heteronomous subjectivations as the "government of conducts" and as a predetermination of the other's range of potential actions are only possible among free subjects who have the option of evading or countering them. Freedom is not only the exercise of resistance to such power relationships, but it is also the pivot point between government of self and government of others. In this sense, the *practice* of freedom is always twofold. It is both critical and creative. It implies questioning of the political-normative framework into which the subject is inserted, as well as a practice of self-transformation. The government of individuals has two modes of exercise: (1) the exterior mode of domination, whereby an individual is subjected to another one's norms and control; and (2) another mode that works through identitarian self-recognition, whereby individuals bind themselves to internalized normative frameworks.

> This form of power applies itself to immediate everyday life which categorizes the individual, mark him by his own individuality, attaches him to his own identity, imposes a law of truth on him which he must recognize and which the others have to recognize in him. It is a form of power which makes individuals subjects. There are two meanings of the word subject: subject to someone else by control and dependence, and tied to his own

identity by a conscience or self-knowledge. Both meanings suggest a form of power which subjugates and makes subject to. (Foucault 1982, 212)

The active exercise of freedom as self-transformation and free subjectivation happens through an action that is at the same time *auto-nomous* and *an-archical*. It is autonomous, because such an action is unbound from the normative framework (*nomos*) the particular regime of truth institutes; it is anarchical because it not determined by the reflectively assumed hetero-produced identity.

Schürmann (1986, 80–81) emphasizes the chiasmatic structure of Foucault's constitution of the practical self. On the one hand, heteronomous subjection takes place through identitarian internalization; on the other hand, the constitution of new forms of subjectivity always happens in a public context. The struggle for subjectivation is autonomous yet external. Schürmann makes two very important points. First, the enforceable normative framework — the specific regime of truth that determines the subjectivation — is an internalized form of identity that precedes all possible autonomous subjectivations. "'Self-identity,' endlessly invoked, thus results from interiorized, although heteronomous, subjection. Self-identity is self-objectivation accepted and enforced as self-subjection" (1986, 303–04). Second, the constitution of the Foucauldian autonomous subject does not occur within an inner space detached from public struggles — it is not a solipsistic process. The affirmation of an autonomous and anarchical subjectivation occurs within the heterogeneous, punctual, and immediate struggles targeting the identitarian effects of those power/knowledge technologies that articulate the individualizing and totalizing aspects of modern governmentality as the secularized form of pastoral power.[24] "They are a refusal of these abstractions, of economic and ideological state violence, which ignore who we are individually, and also a refusal of a scientific or administrative inquisition that determines who one is. To sum up, the main objective of these struggles is to attack not so much 'such or such' institution of power, or group, or elite, or class, but rather a technique, a form of power" (Foucault 1982, 212). Another important and possibly problematic issue that scholars seem to have overlooked concerns the critical mediating function that alterity plays in the subjectivation processes, as well as its coincidence with philosophy's own role. The question about philosophy's task comes to the fore precisely in the transition from the analysis of subjection and heteronomous subjectivation to the inquiry about the possibility of autonomous subjectivation.

Judith Butler emphasized that the regime of truth takes priority over an individual's autonomous possibilities of subjectivation. She argued that the regime of truth defines the normative framework in which ethical recognition takes place, even though "the norms that govern recognition are challenged and transformed" (Butler 2005, 22).[25]

As Deleuze clearly puts it: "There's no subject, but a production of subjectivity: subjectivity has to be produced, when its time arrives, precisely because there is no subject. The time comes once we've worked through knowledge and power; it's that work that force us to frame the new question, it couldn't have been framed before" (Deleuze 1995, 113). This is why the necessary critical mediation that occurs in the transition from an individual's internalized heteronomous subjectivity to the autonomous, anarchical subjectivation is one of the most essential elements of Foucault's subjectivation processes' overall dynamics. As a practice that questions the regimes of truth limiting subjectivation, critical thought is the essential prerequisite for any form of resistance, in addition to being an integral component of the practical subject's active exercise of freedom. As Butler pointed out, critique is also a self-reflective exercise. It focuses on the relationship of the individual with itself because critiquing a given regime of truth coincides with a critique of the specific kind of subjectivation that it produced. In other words, the subject cannot question its normative horizon without questioning itself and the way its subjectivity is heteronomically shaped.

The work on the self evoked by the ancient ascetic practices allows individuals to question their subjectivity and the identity resulting from their internalization of heteronomous processes of subjectivation. However, the distinct investigations carried out by Foucault in his later years show that he assigned the task of critical mediation to the confrontation with alterity. The choice of a particular philosophical and, therefore, critical *ēthos* changes alterity from a subjecting force into an emancipatory one.[26] The philosophical *ēthos* is the product of an autonomous and *an-archical* subjectivation that the philosopher can deploy thanks to ethical reflection as a "reflective practice of freedom." It is a practice that allows philosophers to gain distance from themselves [*se déprendre de soi-même*] and direct their critique to themselves, thereby reactivating the link between philosophy and spirituality that was characteristic of ancient thought.[27] The ensemble of practices and preparatory exercises for the access to *truth* that we call spirituality must be conceived, in this context, as the technique that allows the philosopher to have a relationship with herself mediated by ethical reflection. Foucault gives philosophy — "the critical work that thought brings to bear upon itself" (Foucault 1990, 2:9) — the task of making possible the active exercise of freedom and resistance. Only philosophy seems capable of opening up a space for the constitution of an autonomous and anarchical subjectivation — that is to say, of a subjectivation other with respect to one always already established through the historical hierarchical relationships of power and knowledge.

In other words, we can conclude that the critical mediation of autonomous processes of subjectivation is the task that Foucauldian *practical philosophy* assigns to itself. Such a task amounts to problematizing determined regimes of truth and specific forms of identitarian subjectivation through *an-archaeo-genealogical* critique. It seeks to produce a gap that would eventually warrant the individual's freedom to resist as an autonomously and anarchically constituted subject. At the same time, this philosophical task, coherent with the conceptual horizon to which it belongs, is always practical, contingent, and bound both to the specific context in which it occurs and, most importantly, to the choice to deploy a specific *ēthos* as a virtuous form of acting.

> Significantly, for Foucault — Butler writes — this exposure of the limit of the epistemological field is linked with the practice of virtue, as if virtue is counter to regulation and order, as if the virtue itself is to be found in the risking of established order. [. . .] It belongs to an ethics which is not fulfilled merely by following objectively formulated rules or laws. And virtue is not only a way of complying with or conforming with pre-established norms. It is, more radically, a critical relation to those norms, one which, for Foucault, takes shape as a specific stylization of morality. (2002, 215)

Indeed, within the horizon of *practical philosophy*, ethics can be neither teleological nor deontological. It cannot be grounded upon any universal principle, and it cannot become the object of prescriptions nor a teachable and transmissible doctrine. Rather, in Foucault's thought, ethics coincides with a constant, reflexive, and critical practice aimed at questioning the always contingent boundaries limiting the *ēthos-poietic* freedom that creates "behavioral habits."

We now have a better understanding of Foucault's particular stance towards politics: "Philosophy's question is the question of this present age which is ourselves. This is why philosophy is today entirely political and entirely historical. It is the politics immanent in history and the history indispensable for politics" (Foucault 1996, 222). The widespread misunderstanding of this stance is one of the most apparent results of the interpretations centered on a so-called *turn*, which hold that the relational theory of power and the elaboration of the concept of biopolitics are the core and *apex* of his philosophical quest. Foucault has been read as an essentially political thinker who, in the 1980s, chose to renounce the ideological dimension of his work, move away from politics, and retrieve the spiritual exercises of the ancient tradition for a retreat into philosophical ascesis.[28] I introduced the concept of *practical philosophy* to mark my distance from these interpretations. It is therefore necessary to stress that my reading of Foucault is very far — if not opposed altogether — from those who read his later works on the basis of the idea of *philosophical practice*.[29] Indeed, critics looking to emphasize the importance of Foucault's 1980s works have deemed his re-proposition of the ancient tradition of spiritual exercises (in the wake of his friend and colleague Pierre Hadot's work) as a desire to reconceive philosophy as philosophical practice — in other words, as an exercise of personal transformation that abandons the political dimension to retreat into the intimate space of interiority. Finally, it is also important to point out that the interpretative perspective of Foucault's *practical philosophy* goes further than the most recent works that highlights the importance of Foucault's latest research and some level of coherence in its philosophical itinerary[30]. This to the extent that such a framework allows us to understand the contribution of Foucault going beyond the traditional division of philosophy into political thought, ethics, epistemology, and aesthetics, which seems to be taken for granted by the vast majority of critical literature.

The previous discussion of the critical mediation of subjectivation processes — besides providing an account of the consistency between Foucault's philosophical outlook and his interpretation of the relationship between philosophy and politics — brings two problematic aspects of his *practical philosophy* to the fore.

First of all, the space for the autonomous subjectivation that the *an-archical* actions may produce requires that the philosopher attends to the necessary critical task. It follows that the active exercise of freedom is seemingly subordinated to the contingent possibility of *philosophical heroism*. It is possible — at least in principle — that any individual, once emancipated, may be such a hero because it is only in virtue of a specific, *parrhēsiastic ētho*s that the philosophical alterity may carry out the emancipatory mediation. However, at the same time, the singular, virtuous, and *an-archical* character of free acting and its location within a practical, nonnormative ethics makes it just as fragile and contingent as the regimes of truth they oppose. Since the regime of truth is the historical a priori that every emancipatory attempt must struggle with, it may seem that the space for the active exercise of freedom as autonomous, *an-archical* subjectivation opened up by Foucault's *practical philosophy* is rather narrow and, inevitably, also provisional and risky. It is not by chance that risk is one of the features of *parrhēsia*.[31]

A second problematic aspect concerns the consequences of such philosophical heroism. We may doubt whether the necessary philosophical mediation of processes of subjectivation entails an *aristocratic* perspective. Foucault stresses that he is not suggesting a pedagogical mediation, which would become subjugating in and of itself. Nonetheless, it would not seem impossible that advancing the figure of the *parrhēsiastic* philosopher as the guide of the emancipatory process of an individual or group of individuals may risk introducing a new source of heteronormativity, thanks to the philosopher's inevitable status and its related prestige. Indeed, as I discuss below in the context of his *Collège de France* lectures on *parrhēsia*,[32] Foucault was well aware of this risk and carefully examined the problems that the exercise of *parrhēsia* in a democracy may entail and that Plato and Aristotle had already pointed out. I return to both problematic aspects in the last chapter.

Here, I provided an outline of the philosophical horizon of Foucault's thought, sketched the context from which it originated, and argued that we may refer to it *turning to* the expression *practical philosophy*. The next three chapters leverage the idea of *practical philosophy* to provide a diachronical account of the salient moments of the late developments of Foucault's itinerary, closing the hermeneutic circle that I proposed earlier. As Heidegger wrote, " . . . we must move in a circle. This is neither *ad hoc* nor deficient. To enter upon this path is the strength, to remain on it the feast of thought — assuming that thinking is a craft" (2002, 2).

2
Power, Biopower, Governmentality

> Power's precisely the nonformal element running between or beneath different forms of knowledge. That's why one talks about a microphysics of power. It's force, and the play of forces, not form. And the way Foucault conceives the play of forces, developing Nietzsche's approach, is one of the most important aspects of his thought. It's a different dimension from that of knowledge, although power and knowledge form concretely indivisible composites.
>
> — Deleuze 1995[1]

In the previous chapter, I introduced the concept of *practical philosophy* as a possible answer to Deleuze's question about the logic of Foucault's thought. To put this interpretive proposal to the test, it is now necessary to show how this idea allows us to understand "what drives him on from one level of things to another" — and here, in particular — "what drives him to discover power behind knowledge" (1995, 84). To prove how, from the perspective of the *practical philosophy*, one can clearly leave behind the common claim of a "radical turn" in Foucault's work leading him to abandon the political dimension of thought, we need to move from a retrospective and comprehensive reading of his thought to a diachronic exposition of the problems that Foucault gradually proposed and developed over the last decade of his life. Thus, this chapter shows how the issue of power arose and imposed itself as a central theme throughout Foucault's thought in the 1970s, how it was critically and positively articulated, and finally how and why Foucault came to develop the notion of governmentality.[2] By examining the different stages, the successive conceptual adjustments, and the various critical goals — that is, by following Foucault's rather tortuous path throughout these years — I show that Foucault kept the direction of *practical philosophy* in sight and never lost his orientation even when he seemingly departed from it. This chapter is particularly concerned with the second axis of Foucault's research: the analysis of the strategic relationships between individuals, technologies, and the intersubjective dynamics through which power is exercised. This second axis, however, cannot be separated from the first, which was concerned with how individuals subjectivize themselves as subjects of knowledge and find themselves simultaneously objectified in scientific knowledge. The axes of knowledge and power do not join in a systematic and general theory of power. Together, they constitute the historically determined mesh that defines the characteristics of each specific regime of truth. In the essay "The Subject and Power," Foucault asks rhetorically: "Do we need a theory of power? Since a theory assumes a prior objectivation, it cannot be asserted as a basis for analytical work. But the analytical work cannot proceed without an ongoing conceptualization. And this conceptualization implies critical thought — a constant checking" (Foucault 1982, 209). The knowledge-power pair and the concept of government of truth are precisely two of the forms of conceptualization that Foucault needs for an *an-archaeo-genealogical* analysis of the normative framework of the processes of subjectivation.

A Critical Perspective on the Relational Paradigm of Power

In 1984, to explain how the knowledge-power pair had emerged, Foucault referred back to the placement of the "insane" subject within a game of truth defined by medical knowledge and to the limits of a possible interpretation in terms of ideology.

> In fact, there were practices — essentially the widespread use of incarceration which had been developed starting at the beginning of the seventeenth century, and had been the condition for the insertion of the mad subject in this type of truth game — that sent me back to the problem of institutions of power much more than to the problem of ideology. This is what led me to pose the problem of knowledge and power, which for me is not the fundamental problem but an instrument that makes it possible to analyze the problem of the relationship between subject and truth in what seems to me the most precise way. (Foucault 1997a, 290)

As I mentioned previously, in the 1970s Foucault manifested some incredulity toward his inability to make the issue of power explicit in *History of Madness* or *The Birth of the Clinic*, since such an issue was certainly already implicated in both fields of investigation. The 1973 to 1974 course at the *Collège de France* offers a privileged point of view to sketch out the critical context from which the Foucauldian paradigm of power began to take shape. It is the course dedicated to *Psychiatric Power* (2006a), and it is necessarily connected to his previous research on psychiatry. As it clearly emerges in the first lecture, however, Foucault describes the link fundamentally in terms of discontinuity, in particular with respect to *History of Madness* (2006b).

Right when he is about to resume the thematic path interrupted at the end of *History of Madness*, his first self-criticism concerns his assumption of the perspective of "an analysis of representations" and his narrow focus on what he also calls a "history of mentalities." He had considered the phenomenon of madness only from the different images that the seventeenth- and eighteenth-centuries' tradition provided and from the models of knowledge that were built around it: "The apparatus of power as a productive instance of discursive practice" was missing altogether, he comments (Foucault 2006, 13). The archaeological analysis of a discursive knowledge of psychiatry lacked the genealogical perspective that would identify the context of strategic relations and technologies of power generating such knowledge. In order to question the historical constitution of a "mad" subjectivity — that is, the constitution of the processes of subjectivation of the madman — Foucault has to provide an account of its objectivation in specific, historically determined knowledges and discourses, as well as an analysis of its subjection through specific apparatuses of power. Only then could he show their mutual influences and their reciprocal feedback. Only the *an-archaeo-genealogical* "practical" thought discussed in the previous chapter can accomplish such a task.

The second aspect of Foucault retrospective self-criticism concerns the use of the notion of violence. While this term highlighted the physical aspect of psychiatric power, it almost concealed its strategic organization, and it assumed that its negativity must be entirely attributed to the use of such physicality. Power is violent because it is part and parcel of the same, rationally regulated, strategic functioning of the psychiatric apparatus: "Taken in its final ramifications, at its capillary level, where it affects the individual himself, this power is physical and, thereby, it is violent, in the sense that it is absolutely irregular, not in the sense that it is unbridled, but in the sense, rather, that it is commanded by all the dispositions of a kind of microphysics of bodies" (Foucault 2006, 14). Finally, Foucault distances himself from his previous uses of the notion of institution and the model of the family. He recognizes that through the notion of institution he was implicitly assuming a specific subject, the community, and the rules governing it. This way he had forgone the chance to question the community and its internal dynamics with respect to their own historical constitution as the result of determinate power relations. Similarly, by assuming the family as the model of the asylum, he missed the chance to analyze how the strategies of power-knowledge actually work.

In the course about *Psychiatric Power*, as well as those devoted to *The Punitive Society* (1972–73) and *Abnormal* (1974–75), and *Discipline and Punish* (published in 1975), Foucault tests the critical-philosophical potential of the knowledge-power pair through a series of specific historical investigations of criminal procedure, of the institutionalization and evolution of psychiatry, and of the history of sexuality:

> I always come up against the question of power, a question that no theoretical system — whether the philosophy of history or a general theory of society, or even a political theory — seems able to deal with. That is, those facts of power, those power mechanisms, those power relations at work in the problem of madness, of medicine, of prison, and so on. I have been trying to grapple with that bundle of empirical and poorly elucidated things which power relations consist of, taking them as something that needed explaining. [. . .] But no one has ever accounted for it. I advance one step at a time, examining different domains in succession, to see how a general conception of the relations between the establishment of a knowledge and the exercise of power might be formulated. (Foucault 2001c, 284)

To paraphrase what Foucault said in the introduction to *The Use of Pleasures* about his research on the history of sexuality, these are historical works without being the work of an historian. They "are studies of 'history' by reason of the domain they deal with and the references they appeal to" (1990, 2:9), but their stakes are philosophical. They constitute a philosophical exercise of historical problematization that responds to the need of questioning the patterns, forms of conditioning, and limits that are proper to a particular regime of truth to which thought belongs. Only through such a questioning, thought can actually accede to the freedom of thinking otherwise.

Somehow, we can understand Foucault's dissatisfaction in the first few lines of the course *Society Must Be Defended* (1975–76), when he directly refers to the research he carried out during the first five years of his tenure at the *Collège de France*. Those studies, he says, "were very closely interrelated but [. . .] never added up to a coherent body of work, [. . .] had no continuity. Fragments of research, none of which was completed, and none of which was followed through. Bits and pieces of research, and at the same time it was getting very repetitive, always falling into the same rut, the same themes, the same concepts" (Foucault 2020, 3). Nonetheless, these studies contained a meticulous analysis of disciplinary power, which would help Foucault outline his relational conception of power in later years. They also help us to recognize some equally important critical points about the outcomes of Foucault's inquiry.

In these years, when addressing the issue of disciplinary power as a specific form of power that overlaps and replaces the older form of monarchical sovereignty, Foucault begins to distance himself from the traditional way of thinking about power on the basis of the sovereignty model. In his course on *Psychiatric Power*, he does not present sovereignty as the general model for an ontological conception of power, but rather as a historical mode of power dominant at the time when the disciplinary mode was developed and organized.[3] Before eventually replacing it in the historical hierarchical articulation of different modes of exercising power, disciplinary coexists and meshes with sovereign power: from the post-feudal stage to the nineteenth century, discipline is the *microphysics* of a power that *macrophysically* presents itself as sovereign. This long-standing overlap is made possible by the radical functional differences between the two forms of power. First, sovereign power is necessarily exercised within the dualistic and asymmetrical relationship between subjects and sovereign in the form of the levy. Second, the establishment of such a relationship of sovereignty is always determined by a previous foundational act, be it a divine investiture, an act of conquest, or a voluntary submission in exchange for protection. Third, individual subjects, when confronting sovereign power, can only function as such by subsuming their individual somatic singularities into an indifferent multiplicity. Finally, the exercise of sovereign power does not occur through the classification of hierarchical relationships. To the contrary, disciplinary power is exercised analytically through the hierarchization of a series of relations directed at the uninterrupted coercion of individuals through their bodies. These procedures sought a constant and permanent control of individual actions and bodily movements in view of the economic management of forces. The individual body can now be placed, moved, and articulated upon others. Each individual's time must agree with the others' in order to extract from each the greatest possible amount of force and combine it into the best possible outcome. The absorption of individuals into society's productive apparatus is at stake.

Disciplinary power demands a precise system of command, yet it should not be identified with a certain institution: it is a mode, a technology of exercising power that can be absorbed within a previously existing macro-mechanism of power, such as sovereign power. From this perspective Foucault considers discipline as the principle of the actual functioning of psychiatric power and the penal system, as well as of military apparatuses and pedagogical institutions.

The studies of these years clearly show that Foucault is interested in a theory of power as *micro-physics*, although it would be more accurately called *micro-dynamics*. Foucault is more interested in the micro-mechanisms at work in individuals' material processes of subjugation than in a general and universal theory of power that would presuppose the subject as a given. Only the analysis of the micro-mechanisms that act within the formal limits of power established by law enables inquiry into the "modes" of power and questions the effects of truth they produce, which in turn preserve and strengthen them. In fact, the effects of truth concern the real and effective practices of power. It is power considered in the widespread exercise that permeates individuals' experiences and constitutes them as subjects, rather than power conceived as a unitary and homogeneous phenomenon dominating a community of subjects through law. Only an analysis that considers the actual plural dynamics of power at work in specific contexts of subjection can provide an account of the interdependence between the effects of domination and those of knowledge. Only an analysis that approaches power from a *practical*, functional, and — above all — historical perspective can account for the actual mechanisms of subjectivation.

Clearly, this perspective does not consider power as a negative instance — that is, it does not start from repression as power's fundamental function. The critique of the notion of repression appears in the second lesson of the course on *Abnormal*, and it especially plays a central role in the first volume of *The History of Sexuality* and at the beginning of the course *Society Must Be Defended* (1975–76). The interpretation of power as being mainly repressive is the chief polemical target of Foucault's analysis. On the contrary, he seeks to highlight power's positive and productive dimension. The focus on repression reinforces a simplistic and skeletal vision of power that reduces its entire dynamics to a purely limiting and negative function — namely, the determination of the licit/illicit alternative. This perspective enjoys an undisputed consensus, as Foucault repeatedly stresses. He confesses the difficulties he encountered while trying to get rid of this notion. He used it implicitly in *History of Madness* before he thematized the question of power because "it does indeed appear to correspond so well with a whole range of phenomena that belong among the effects of power" (Foucault 2001c, 119). The reason behind such success is undoubtedly tied to the political advantage implied by this idea. As Foucault explains in the course of the debate following the conference "Sexuality and Power," held in Tokyo on April 20, 1978, the identification of power with a repressive instance offers an immediate advantage, for the mere, hoped-for abolition of a prohibition would amount to a full conquest of freedom. Foucault's departure from the paradigm of repressive power occurs when his studies of the disciplines and the systems of surveillance and punishment in Western societies between the eighteenth and nineteenth centuries led him to realize the essentially productive character of the disciplining of individuals.

In the course at the *Collège de France* in 1974 to 1975, the issue emerges from the analysis of a series of mechanisms of power that are orthogonal to the areas of research on which he recently had dwelt. Foucault calls them mechanisms of *normalizing* power. They do not properly belong to either the legal or the medico-psychiatric institutions, but rather to the borderland between the two. Foucault introduces the analysis of the mechanisms of normalization precisely through the thematization of medico-legal expertise, insofar as it represents the junction between the judicial and the medical domains that is heterogeneous to both law and medicine. In medico-legal expertise, both law and psychiatry are taken out of their element and face a different horizon of subjectivation. They are no longer confronted with the sick vs. sane or the guilty vs. innocent oppositions, but by the normal vs. abnormal one. Thus, medico-legal expertise brings a different type of power into play. This is a power that presents itself as a controlling instance of the abnormal individual and slowly transforms both psychiatric knowledge and judicial power while establishing an increasingly tighter connection between them. Normalizing power does not set in motion mechanisms of marginalization, exclusion, or repression, but rather it elicits mechanisms of inclusion, control, and meticulous observation through which it directly, positively, and productively takes charge of the processes of subjectivation of individuals. We must look to these kinds of mechanisms, Foucault explains, to understand how power has acted in the realm of sexuality. A close scrutiny of the negative conception of power as repression becomes urgent precisely when we interrogate sexuality and test the knowledge-power pair in the field of sexual behavior.

What Foucault calls the "repressive hypothesis" belongs to the psychoanalytic perspective that Freud and many of his successors offer and whom Foucault generally refers to as Freudo-Marxists.[4] In fact, the repressive hypothesis is not completely foreign to Foucault's inquiry, insofar as it seeks to clarify the active role power relations play in the processes of subjectivation of individuals. This contiguity is, however, precisely what makes the Foucauldian distancing necessary. The repressive hypothesis plays in the hands of power by assigning a central role to censorship and prohibition, while concealing power's productive aspects. It allows itself to be manipulated by the internal cunning of power's own mechanisms and becomes an unconscious instrument of subjugation. Foucault does not intend to deny the existence of sexual prohibitions. He wants to shift the focus of the analysis from silences and prohibitions to the instances of positive power-knowledge that produce and impose them.

The discussion of the repressive hypothesis must be connected to Foucault's criticism of Marxism and of the ontological conception of power on the model of sovereignty, which he explored in depth from 1975 to 1976. Foucault holds that the attribution to political power of a purely negative function is, in fact, analogous to the idea that political power is a mere superstructure whose only function is the preservation of the structural relations of production. From Foucault's point of view, Marxism presupposes the essential unity of political power and identifies it with the power of legal interdiction that is exercised on given subjects. Marxism remains captive to the threefold presupposition that grounds the theory of sovereignty — namely, the presupposition of unity, of the subject, and of the law:

> Sovereign, law, and prohibition formed a system of representation of power which was extended during the subsequent era by the theories of right: political theory has never ceased to be obsessed with the person of the sovereign. Such theories still continue today to busy themselves with the problem of sovereignty. What we need, however, is a political philosophy that isn't erected around the problem of sovereignty or, therefore, around the problems of law and prohibition. We need to cut off the king's head. In political theory that has still to be done. (Foucault 2001d, 122)

Foucault does not intend to set aside the important role that the state and the legal exercise of state power play. His point is that state apparatuses and laws cover only a minimal part of the field of real and pre-existing power relations on which the state depends.

Foucault's analysis of disciplines and normalization or, rather, his analysis of the system of normalizing disciplines, describes this field of multiform and mobile relations where the norm produces effects of subjectivation allowing for a precise control over the individual, for a continuous and strategic dialectic between power and knowledge, and between power and truth.

This first cycle of Foucauldian research on the question of power can be considered concluded with *Society Must Be Defended* (1975–76). These studies were strongly linked to the "locations" of disciplinary power and were tied to the political context and to the "dispersed and discontinuous offensives" that were taking place then (I am referring to the militant experience of the GIP and the problematization of the themes the anti-psychiatric movement was debating, in which Foucault was only marginally involved),[5] and they culminated in the experience of *Discipline and Punish*. In a note concluding *Society Must Be Defended*, which was held between the publication of the book on the birth of the prison and that of the first volume of *The History of Sexuality* (i.e., *The Will to Know*), the editors write: "This course occupies a specific, one might say strategic, position in Foucault's thought and research. It marks a sort of pause, a momentary halt and no doubt a turning point, in which he evaluates the road that he has traveled and outlines future lines of investigation" (Foucault 2003b, 273 modified).

The dissatisfaction clearly manifested by Foucault in the first lines of the course certainly concerns the need to restore dignity to his whole project. But it also shows the need to redraw the critical horizon of intellectual militancy and philosophical work. With the disappearance of power-enacted repression as the horizon of sense, the urgency to foreground and un-conceal specific knowledges or specific local discourses is also lost. Foucault is neither concerned with trying to overcome the fragmentary nature of the investigations he conducted, nor is he concerned with their insertion into a system organized according to a theoretical principle. It is not a matter of inserting these "dispersed genealogies" into the framework of a new general theory of power, as Dreyfus and Rabinow would have it. Rather, it is a matter of restoring some coherence to the research being carried out, and to start from a determinate critical perspective, while keeping a steady focus on a philosophical horizon that is increasingly becoming clearer. The course proceeds precisely in this direction.

According to Foucault, the legal-liberal conception of political power and Marxism have in common a perspective that he defines as "economicist." In fact, the former understands power as a right that is owned as a commodity would be. Each individual holds it exactly like a commodity and they would surrender it through contracts, either totally or partially, in order to constitute political sovereignty, thereby setting up an obvious analogy between power and wealth. In Marxist theory, however, power has an economic function because its role is to preserve the relations of production and the class domination they produce — that is, power is subordinated to the economy and finds its historical and concrete ground in it. In the legal-liberal conception, economy and politics are linked by a formal isomorphism; in Marxism, they are connected by a functional subordination. Is it possible, Foucault asks, to formulate a non-economic analysis of power? Evidently, the answer lies in the relational conception of power that he was trying to articulate in previous years.

Power is not a commodity — it is not acquired, accumulated, traded, or relinquished. Power, argues Foucault, is a relationship of force that is exercised and exists only when it is concretely carried out. It exists in the network of relationships that binds individuals to each other and places them in a situation of mutual dependence and mutual production with respect to the truth. Therefore, the analysis of power cannot be ontological: it must be dynamic and must describe the *how*, the mechanics of power. This *how* cannot be understood as a repressive exercise — or more generally the negative mechanism of prohibition through the opposition between licit and illicit — because such a mechanism cannot provide an account of the positive bond between power and practices of truth.

Another possible answer to the question of the mechanics of power relations is the Nietzschean suggestion about the warlike model of power, which by overturning Clausewitz's well-known thesis, argues that power is war continued by other means — that is, it is the maintenance of the disequilibrium between forces manifested in war. Foucault puts this model to the test in *Society Must Be Defended* as a possible interpretative paradigm of relations of domination. Lesson after lesson, he retraces the different theoretical formulations that, over the course of four centuries, have turned war into the matrix of power relations and used it as an interpretative grid to read historical-political reality:[6] "In short, and unlike the philosophico-juridical discourse organized around the problem of sovereignty and the law, the discourse that deciphers war's permanent presence within society is essentially a historico-political discourse, a discourse in which truth functions as a weapon to be used for a partisan victory, a discourse that is darkly critical and at the same time intensely mythical" (Foucault 2003b, 270).

The discourse, whose authorship can be attributed neither to Hobbes nor to Clausewitz, has had an immense number of popular and anonymous champions, including the racist and eugenicist biologists of the late twentieth century.[7] These theories, as opposed to the philosophical-juridical one, argue that political power does not begin when war ceases. First, war can never be averted because it presided over the birth of states. Jurisprudence, peace, and laws were born from the blood and mud of battles — actual massacres, not philosophers' ideal concoctions. It is war that is the engine of institutions and order: peace, even in its most infinite mechanisms, silently makes war. A battlefront, a binary structure runs through society as a whole: there is no neutral subject, we are necessarily opponents of someone. From this perspective, freedom is mostly a function of being able to subtract it or appropriate from another: it is the exact opposite of equality. "[Freedom] is something that is enjoyed thanks to difference, domination, and war, thanks to a whole system of relations of force. A freedom that cannot be translated into a nonegalitarian relationship of force can only be a freedom that is weak, impotent, and abstract" (Foucault 2003b, 157).

Foucault stresses the strategic polyvalence of the interpretation of reality from a war perspective. Since its origin at the end of the Middle Ages, this discourse was never bound to a specific context. It has never functioned in one and only one political sense. Rather, it has demonstrated a great ability to mutate and circulate. And precisely for this reason it could provide a theoretical framework for the revolutionary theory of class struggle as well as biological racism. Moreover, it is an analysis that has played a fundamental role in the development of historical discourse. It is an important discourse because it overturns the traditional polarities of intelligibility by demanding an explanation from below. Above all, it develops entirely within the historical realm, without trying to tie the relativity of history to the absolutes of law and truth. Its grounding principle is the binary structure of its analysis: the social body is composed of two distinct and opposed sets in a relationship of permanent war. The state is just how they continue to conduct their war in seemingly pacific ways.

However, the interest of the warlike interpretation of power relations lies, for Foucault, in its strategic perspective and in the idea of struggle, rather than its binary logic. The field of power relations is configured as a complex set of heterogeneous and punctual oppositions and resistances. Foucault seeks to work out an interpretive paradigm that may account for this complexity without universalizing or substantializing it. The knowledge-power pair was an important first step in this direction, for it was especially effective from the critical point of view. Yet it was not completely satisfactory, nor completely exhaustive. On the other hand, the paradigm of war is too closely linked to binary logic to offer an account of the countless local and contingent struggles. It can neither serve as an integration, nor is it a key to reading the micro-dynamics of power relations. It is, in fact, a paradigm that evolves within the historical discourse and becomes intertwined with the development of the idea of nation, thereby grounding the very possibility of a philosophy of history, and making possible the birth of dialectics: "What took place there was a self-dialecticization of historical discourse, and it occurred independently of any explicit transposition — or any explicit utilization — of a dialectical philosophy into a historical discourse" (Foucault 2003b, 237). From the nineteenth century forward, philosophy and history ask the same question about the universal truth that the present carries within itself. Dialectics is born.

Biopower, Discipline, Biopolitics

Given the analytical failure of war paradigm, Foucault's quest for a way to account for the *how* of power and the modalities through which the internal relation of the power-knowledge pair has been historically articulated remains open. We find another attempted answer in the last lecture of the 1975 to 1976 course and, after an almost identical analysis, in the last chapter of *The Will to Know*. It is here that the category of biopolitics is fully developed, alongside the notion of discipline to which Foucault's research had turned in the first half of the 1970s.[8]

In the courses prior to *Society Must Be Defended* and in *Discipline and Punish*, Foucault had contrasted disciplinary power with sovereignty, while describing it as a mechanism that may and does indeed begin to function within the same macro-figure of sovereign power, even though it ends up prevailing. Foucault did not, however, provide further clarifications about the historical evolution of the macro-physical level nor of the articulation of one level on the other. In 1976, he outlines a historical and theoretical framework that seems to give him the organic unity whose absence he had regretted and that, in retrospect, will help him introduce the notion of *government*. The idea of *government* plays a crucial role in the elucidation of power relations' mechanics and, most importantly, in the articulation of the different aspects of the practical constitution of subjectivity — that is, the articulation of the three dimensions of the processes of subjectivation.

Foucault argues that the mechanisms of power undergo a radical transformation from the seventeenth century onward: the main forms of power exercise are no longer the "withdrawal," subtraction, submission, or destruction that were typical of sovereignty. Rather, power comes to be exercised through mechanisms of surveillance, augmentation, and organization of the vital forces that it subdues. The right to death becomes the other face of a power that is positively and productively exercised over life. Foucault calls this new mechanism *biopower*. In concrete terms, biopower is articulated in two main forms, neither antithetical nor simultaneous to each other.

The first form corresponds to disciplinary power, or as Foucault calls it here, to the *anatomo-politics of the human body* that emerged in the classical age, as we saw above. The second form is the *biopolitics of population*, which would emerge instead towards the middle of the eighteenth century.[9] On the one hand, then, we find a discipline that is exercised on the body of man as an individual-machine, which must ensure an organization as economical as possible, as well as a constant control and a spatial distribution, in addition to training and empowerment. On the other hand, we see a biopolitics that is exercised on the body-species and the population, in the form of management and regulation of biological processes such as a population's proliferation, its birth and mortality rates, its level of health, life span, and longevity. Discipline and biopolitics, however, are the two faces of biopower that remain separate and autonomous until the nineteenth century, when their connection is finally established through a whole series of newly emerging technologies of power-knowledge: " . . . for millennia, man remained what he was for Aristotle: a living animal with the additional capacity for a political existence; modern man is an animal whose politics places his existence as a living being in question" (Foucault 1978c, 143).

From this standpoint, the life of such a living being, whose responsibility biopower has assumed, is understood in two different ways according to the different technologies of discipline and biopolitics. In the disciplinary context, life is at stake in the broad sense of the existence of individuals whose organic bodies carry determinate forces and specific capacities. Power seeks to control these bodies' behaviors through surveillance and training. The life that biopolitical technologies have as their object is conceived as the collective biological life of the *human mass* of the population that power attempts to regulate through a series of biological and bio-sociological knowledges. Statistical and demographic estimates as well as biopolitical mechanisms seek to intervene at the level of general biological phenomena. The dynamics of *normalization*, which Foucault discussed in 1974 to 1975, joins the two forms of biopower's concrete exercise. Power is carried out as a norm when disciplining the body as well as when regulating the population, and it always starts from a primarily medical and hygienic knowledge. A power that wants to take charge of life through corrective mechanisms and continuous reinforcements cannot refer to the system of law because the law sanctions the difference between what is licit and what is illicit starting from the threat of death characteristic of sovereign power:

> The normalizing society is a society in which the norm of discipline and the norm of regulation intersect along an orthogonal articulation. To say that power took possession of life in the nineteenth century, or to say that power at least takes life under its care in the nineteenth century is to say that it has, thanks to the play of technologies of discipline on the one hand and technologies of regulation on the other, succeeded in covering the whole surface that lies between the organic and the biological, between body and population. (Foucault 2003b, 253)

Whether it is the individual or collective exercise of power — that is, whether it is a disciplinary or biopolitical mode of power — this exercise always brings into play specific strategies of knowing and targets a determinate constitution of subjectivity. When disciplining individuals and when biopolitically regulating them through a referral to their belonging to a biological species, biopower enacts a form of subjectivation as an identity that presupposes something like *nature* and is administered by a medical, rather than legal, knowledge. The subject is assigned a specific identity on the basis of particular *natural* characteristics according to the criteria established by the norms. The subject is assigned and reduced to an identity that is presumed to be its *natural* biological truth, and its sexual behavior or its presumed racial characteristics are considered symptoms — that is, exterior manifestations of such a profound truth.

The apparatus of sexuality provides both the continuity and the ideal connection between the two technologies of biopower. In fact, sex is subject to the individualizing control of the disciplines as behavior of the individual body, while as procreation, it is included among those biological processes affecting the biopolitics of the population.[10] Thus, the analysis of the apparatus of sexuality allows Foucault to target the articulation of the two modes of exercising biopower (discipline and biopolitics), while making explicit the terms of the relationship in the power-knowledge pair. Foucault shows that what is at stake in sex is, precisely, the subjectivation of individuals. His analysis makes clear that the Christian technology of confession lies at the heart of the apparatus of sexuality. The institute of confession is both a paradigmatic example of a practice of truth entirely traversed by relations of power and a self-reflexive modality of the subject: "The confession is a ritual of discourse in which the speaking subject is also the subject of the statement; it is also a ritual that unfolds within a power relationship, for one does not confess without the presence (or virtual presence) of a partner who is not simply the interlocutor but the authority who requires the confession, prescribes and appreciates it, and intervenes in order to judge, punish, forgive, console, and reconcile" (Foucault 1978c, 61). The clinical coding of confessions as a performative discursive ritual, the medicalization of their effects, the institutionalization of the method of interpretation, and the positing of sexuality's intrinsic latency translates sexual confessions into scientific forms and makes possible the development of a *scientia sexualis*. Confession becomes a technology of objectivation of the subject and a mechanism of identitarian subjectivation. The confession ritual offers a privileged perspective on the relationship between truth and the constitution of subjectivity, and so, it occupies a prominent position among the different sex-related technologies of power-knowledge that Foucault examines. This is precisely why confession also plays a fundamental role in the development of the concept of government.[11]

The analysis of biopower undoubtedly also responds to the need to offer an alternative to the Marxist interpretation of the relations between power and economy that Foucault criticized on several occasions and from which he tried to distance himself. He contends that power relations are not subordinate to economic relations: and, therefore, they cannot be explained from the standpoint of economics. Not only can power relations not be reduced to the mere function of preserving economic relations; but also, on the contrary, biopower is one of the conditions of possibility for the development of capitalism: "The investment of the living body, its valorization and the distributive management of its forces were at the time indispensable" (Foucault 1978c, 141). The mechanisms of disciplinary subjugation of individuals, and their inclusion in a hierarchical system of "economic" management of their bodies made the capitalist organization of labor possible. Disciplinary technologies act at the level of economic processes by intervening directly on the productive forces.

The relationship between the second technology of biopower (i.e., biopolitics), and the economy is obviously more complex. Foucault addressed this in the 1979 course, in whose manuscript we find a marginal note about biopolitics: "But who does not see that this is only part of something much larger, which

[is] this new governmental reason? Studying liberalism as the general framework of biopolitics" (Foucault 2010, 22).

Government and Governmentality

Foucault's next two courses at the *Collège de France* — *Security, Territory, Population* (1977–78) and *The Birth of Biopolitics* (1978–79) — published simultaneously, are "a diptych unified by the problematic of biopower" (Foucault 2007b, 477) that offer a chance to dig deeper into the themes that had emerged at the end of the previous course. Foucault could now bring the analysis of the procedures and strategies that he had tried to gather under the concept of biopower to a more adequate development. In this context, Foucault starts testing the concept that, from 1979 to 1980 and onward, replaces the power-knowledge pair as the key conceptual tool of his research. It is in these pages that the notion of government appears for the first time.

Here more than elsewhere, the experimental character of Foucault's lectures appears in full light. The deep continuity that unites these courses concerns mostly the provisional character of their assumptions and the dynamism of thought in its own becoming, for we witness one of the most significant and fruitful *déplacements* of Foucault's philosophical itinerary. Only if we grasp its meaning can we reject the interpretation that locates the political checkmate of Foucault's thought in these years and presents them as the preparatory move before the great turn projecting him into the sphere of subjective ethics.

Such a perspective shift occurs slowly over the course of two years of lectures. Foucault intended to resume and clarify all those issues that had emerged — and that he often had barely hinted at — when he advanced the notion of biopower as the framework for the micro-physical analysis of disciplines next to the macro-physical level of the *biopolitics of population*. Indeed, the 1977 to 1978 course begins with these words:

> This year I would like to begin studying something that I have called, somewhat vaguely, biopower. By this I mean a number of phenomena that seem to me to be quite significant, namely, the set of mechanisms through which the basic biological features of the human species became the object of a political strategy, of a general strategy of power, or, in other words, how, starting from the eighteenth century, modern western societies took on board the fundamental biological fact that human beings are a species. (Foucault 2007b, 16)

The analysis of the title — *Security, Territory, Population* — clarifies the terms of the first movement through which Foucault seeks to approach a clarification of the historical articulation of the two modes of biopower. In fact, *security* refers to an apparatus of power that is not exercised over a *territory*, but directed toward a *population*, to which biopolitics must be referred. The security apparatus gathers, transforms, and integrates both the legal mechanism that sanctions the division between licit and illicit, and the disciplinary mechanism of surveillance and correction of the *abnormal*. With respect to the previous analyses, Foucault specifies that the disciplines give priority to the norm sanctioning the normal-abnormal distinction. One should therefore speak of *normation* rather than *normalization*, with the latter term being better suited to security apparatuses.[12] Indeed, security techniques examine events in their concrete nature and seek to regulate them, to bring them back to more favorable and more normal levels. They always act within reality itself and take their start from notions such as chance, risk, danger, and crisis. Here: "The norm is an interplay of differential normalities. The normal comes first and the norm is deduced from it, or the norm is fixed and plays its operational role on the basis of this study of normalities" (Foucault 2007b, 91). Security represents the political correlate of the economic principles of liberalism, whose analysis Foucault tackles the following year. The subject-object of these technologies of security is the population,[13] which is no longer understood as a set of individuals belonging to a given territory; rather, it is seen as a natural phenomenon that exhibits several observable constant parameters, biological or otherwise, in addition to possibly predictable behaviors, desires, and regularities that may even cover chance occurrences. Foucault states:

> From one direction, then, population is the human species, and from another it is what will be called the public. [. . .] The public, which is a crucial notion in the eighteenth century, is the population seen under the aspect of its opinions, ways of doing things, forms of behavior, customs, fears, prejudices, and requirements; [. . .] The population is therefore everything that extends from biological rootedness through the species up to the surface that gives one a hold provided by the public. (Foucault 2007b, 105)

It is clear that the scope of Foucault's inquiry has broadened since his earlier focus on population as a correlate of biopolitics. From the very first hours of the course, he shows that the complexity brought into play by population as the subject-object of power-knowledge relations goes far beyond the limits of its biological connotations as a biopolitically enacted form of (collective) subjectivation. Moreover, Foucault needs to focus on this complexity to develop an alternative account of the relationship between power and economy with respect to Marxism. Such an account would start from the specific historical form that has allowed, accompanied, and followed the development of capitalism. Foucault connects the transformation of the analysis of wealth, built on the model of family management into political economy, to the emergence of population as subject-object of power-knowledge. At the same time, the structure of the historical framework that he traces becomes increasingly complex, as he removes the implicit dualism of the analysis of biopower, which he had previously carried out on two parallel levels. Responding to the transversality of the concept of population, the security apparatus is the first tool that escapes from this bipartite analysis. The notions of government and governmentality appear for the first time in this context.

On the one hand, the concept of government irrupts in Foucault's discourse as a specific form of power-knowledge. It corresponds to the population considered from the bio-economic-humanistic standpoint that characterizes actuality more comprehensively than the idea of biopolitics. On the other hand, government is a conceptual tool that seems to adapt to the whole spectrum of power relations, thus avoiding the rigidity of the microphysical-macrophysical dualism.

Foucault links the issue of government to the emergence of population as a correlate of power and an object of knowledge that problematizes it, thereby determining the actual opening of the political field. According to Foucault's reading, this occurs, historically speaking, alongside the eighteenth-century demographic expansion and the increasing importance of statistical knowledge.

This is the time when political economy, understood as the science of the relationship between population, territory, and wealth, takes shape. It provides the techniques of government that will assume a dominant role, and it is assigned the task to intervene in the field of population and economy. From the eighteenth century forward, Foucault explains, with the emergence of political science the focus moves from the structures of sovereignty to a regime in which such techniques of government dominate although neither sovereignty nor discipline disappear. What takes place is not a mechanical substitution, but rather a dynamic transformation that settles into a different equilibrium and a different order of priorities. Foucault claims that the accomplished and undisputed dominance of the technologies of government in the political space characterizes our modernity, precisely, as the era of governmentality:

> By the word "governmentality" I mean three things. First, the set of institutions, procedures, analyses and reflections, calculations and tactics that allow for the exercise of this specific and highly complex form of power, which has the population as its main target, political economy as its privileged form of knowledge, and security devices as its essential technical tool. Second, by "governmentality" I mean the tendency, the line of force that throughout the West, for a long time, has continued to assert the pre-eminence of this type of power that we call government over all others — sovereignty, discipline — with the consequent development, on the one hand, of a series of special governmental apparatuses, and, on the other, of a series of forms of knowledge. Finally, "governmentality" must be understood as the process, or rather the result of the process, by which the state of justice of the Middle Ages, which became an administrative state during the fifteenth and sixteenth centuries, found itself gradually governmentalized. (Foucault 2007b, 144)

Foucault actually devotes the next course to the specific analysis of modern governmentality, while the 1977 to 1978 course continues with a twofold genealogical foray that sets the stage for later developments. The first incursion concerns the very concept of the government of men on the basis of the analysis of Christian pastoral care. The second deals with the art of government as an autonomous problem, beginning with the birth of the concept of *raison d'État* in the seventeenth century. A large part of chapter 3 discusses the genealogical inquiry that ties the government of men back to its Christian matrix. In this context, the thematization of *raison d'État* piques Foucault's interests for three different reasons. First, it allows him to test the notion of government against the possibility of a radical critique of the unquestioned centrality of the problem of the state. Second, it is the first instance of a discussion of political government that emphasizes its specificity and uniqueness rather than its continuity with other modes of government. Finally, from a genealogical standpoint, it is the antecedent of modern governmentality and the decisive stage of the process of governmentalization that Foucault wants to examine.

Foucault holds that the overestimation of the problem of the state within political thought affects both those who mythologize its function and those who seemingly assign it a reductive role. In both cases, there is an implicit assumption of unity, abstract individuality, and the decisive importance of the state in power dynamics. Even in this instance, Foucault's critical targets are both classical political philosophy and Marxism. He accuses Marxism of falling into the same theoretical trap of classical philosophy as it repeats the latter's tendency to build political theory on the model of sovereignty. Even when it subordinates the role of the state to the preservation and development of the capitalist structure, Marxism still considers the state as the essential target of political struggle. On the contrary, Foucault intends to show that the state "is only a composite reality and a mythicized abstraction whose importance is much less than we think. Maybe. What is important for our modernity, that is to say for our present, is not then the state's takeover [*étatisation*] of society, so much as what I would call the 'governmentalization' of the state" (Foucault 2007b, 144). The state exists and it exists in its present form as a function of the techniques of government. The fundamental goal of the analyses Foucault pursues on the basis of the concepts of government and governmentality is the application of the same critical mechanism he used on the disciplines to the state:

> In short, the point of view adopted in all these studies involved the attempt to free relations of power from the institution, in order to analyze them from the point of view of technologies; to distinguish them also from the function, so as to take them up within a strategic analysis; and to detach them from the privilege of the object, so as to resituate them within the perspective of the constitution of fields, domains, and objects of knowledge. If this triple movement of a shift to the outside was tried

out with regard to the disciplines, I would now like to explore this possibility with regard to the state. (Foucault 2007b, 164)

The state, like the disciplines, must be "deinstitutionalized," "defunctionalized," and "de-objectivized" in order to develop its genealogy. Only on this basis is it possible to understand the mobile and unstable power relations that crisscross the state as they act. There is no other way, Foucault claims, to regain the continuity between the micro and macro levels of the analysis of power relations. The concept of government offers a particularly suitable framework toward this end, because it is both extremely ductile and strongly biased toward a *practical* meaning. I am referring to the broad sense of the term *practical* I discussed in the previous chapter. In this regard, the course's final words are particularly significant: "Certainly, I do not think analyzing the state as a way of doing things is the only possible analysis when one wants to do the history of the state, but it is, I think, a sufficiently fruitful possibility, and to my mind its fruitfulness is linked to the fact that we can see that there is not a sort of break between the level of micro-power and the level of macro-power, and that talking about one [does not] exclude talking about the other" (Foucault 2007b, 455). Before taking on a properly political value from the sixteenth century onward, the problem of government had already been posed at different levels. The return to Stoicism brought the issue of self-government into play, the government of souls was central to the Catholic and Protestant pastoral care, while finally, the problem of a prince's government of the state also made its appearance.[14] These attempts tried to show the continuity between governing a state and the other forms of government. It is through the theory of the *raison d'État* that the issue of political government becomes independent from all other forms of government.[15]

The *raison d'État* was born between the end of the sixteenth century and the beginning of the seventeenth century.[16] It was perceived as a novelty and even as a scandal from the beginning because it made no reference to anything external to the state as such: neither to a natural nor to a divine order.[17] The *raison d'État* sets up a relation of the state to itself, where the ideal necessity of the state is both a principle of intelligibility and a strategic goal of the governing reason. The reference to the population, though implicit, is not yet in the foreground. In fact, the stance of the *raison d'État* is essentially conservative: it is a matter of getting to know the essence of the state to do what is necessary and sufficient to obey it and to maintain its integrity. Since the goal of this new governing reason is the safety of the state, it is not subordinate to its laws: it respects them in its ordinary exercise only because they are functional to it, but it can always free itself from them when necessary. The *raison d'État* must take into account two decisive elements: the economy and public opinion. The government must be able to manage these two elements of reality if it is to avoid revolts and sedition and obtain obedience; these elements allow the safeguard of the state's strength or the further strengthening it needs to avoid being dominated by others and prevent its disintegration. The fundamental novelty, crucial to the governmentalization framework, is that the object and principle of intelligibility of the *raison d'État* is the force of the states as it unfolds in a field of competing relational forces. This is why increasing the forces of the state is part and parcel of its safeguard.

Historically speaking, the political reason based on the dynamics of forces deploys two fundamental apparatuses: the diplomatic-military apparatus and the police. Both aim at preserving the relation of forces and developing the forces internal to each element — that is, they seek a security mechanism. While the diplomatic-military apparatus strives to keep the European equilibrium in place, the police is — on the other hand — the set of means that will grow the forces of the state and ensure a good order.[18] It is the calculation and the technique that allow for the establishment of a flexible yet still stable and controllable relationship between the internal order of the state and the growth of its forces. On the one hand, according to European equilibrium, the development of police in the individual states must be parallel; on the other hand, the same European equilibrium, as a kind of interstate police, will supervise the good functioning of the police in the individual states. European equilibrium and the police share the instrument of statistics to decipher the constituent forces of the various states. Seeking to control and take charge of human activity as a constitutive element of the force of the state, the police apparatus sets in motion the transformations for which the new form of subjectivation of the population is born: "If the governmentality of the state is interested, for the first time, in the fine materiality of human existence and coexistence, of exchange and circulation [. . .] it is because at that time commerce is thought of as the main instrument of the state's power and thus as the privileged object of a police whose objective is the growth of the state's forces" (Foucault 2007b, 440). With respect to the art of governing by *raison d'État*, the diplomatic-military apparatus operates as foreign policy's self-regulating mechanism. The correlate of these limitations in international relations is the absence of limits in the exercise of the police state.

The fundamental transformation that gives modern governmentality its specific characters is played out on the issue of the limits of governmental practice, around the middle of the eighteenth century. Foucault devotes his course *The Birth of Biopolitics* (1978–79) to the analysis of this transformation and the new rationality of the governmental art that ensues, which coincides with what is generally called *liberalism*. Foucault explains the seemingly complete discrepancy with the course's title at the end of the first lesson: " . . . only when we know what this governmental regime called liberalism was, will we be able to grasp what biopolitics is" (Foucault 2010, 22). In other words, we can only analyze the technology of biopolitical power if we start from the general regime of power-knowledge or, to put it better, start from the regime of government from which it was born — namely, liberalism.

Foucault claims that we must consider the new liberal art of government as an internal refinement of the *raison d'État*, which it improves and brings to a fuller development. The transformation consists essentially of instituting a principle of limitation at the very core of the practice of government. Self-limitation becomes the internal principle regulating government's rationality: "The whole question of critical governmental reason will turn on how not to govern too much. The objection is no longer to the abuse of sovereignty but to excessive government" (Foucault 2010, 13). With the advent of liberalism, the principle of maximum/minimum replaces the notion of equal justice and the opposition between licit and illicit. In short, liberalism installs the principle of government's self-limitation as the emerging regime of truth.

Political economy is the intellectual tool, the form of rationality that enables the self-limitation and self-regulation of governmental action. Political economy does not develop independently or even against the *raison d'État* — on the contrary, its goals are consistent with the objectives that the *raison d'État* had determined to be appropriate for the art of government. In fact, the objective of political economy is the simultaneous, correlated, and properly regulated growth of the population and its means of subsistence. Its goal is to keep some amount of balance among the states that would allow competition. Political economy tries to detect the existence of phenomena and regularities that intelligible and necessary mechanisms produce, which may be hindered by governmental practices. First of all, political economy starts from the assumption that governmental practice must respect the nature of its objects and operations: "In short, through political economy there is the simultaneous entry into the art of government of, first, the possibility of self-limitation, that is, of governmental action limiting itself by reference to the nature of what it does and of that on which it is brought to bear, [and second, the question of truth]" (Foucault 2010, 17).

Second, political economy indicates to government that it should look at the market as the proper *locus* containing the truth principle of its specific practice. Until the eighteenth century, the market was the *locus* of distributive justice, and it had to be maintained through strict regulation. By the middle of the eighteenth century, the market is represented as having to obey natural mechanisms, which must be understood to avoid altering their course. Since prices are a result of the market's natural mechanisms, they become a criterion of truth that may distinguish between right and wrong governmental practices.

Foucault highlights the fundamental traits of liberalism — the market as truth criterion, the determination of the limits of the utility of government through calculation, and, finally, the establishment of Europe as a region of unlimited economic development in relation to a world market. But he stresses that they refer to a much more general phenomenon than mere economic doctrine. It is a reality "in which economic processes and institutional framework call on each other, support each other, modify and shape each other in ceaseless reciprocity" (Foucault 2010, 164). Foucault is interested in analyzing capitalism as a historical legal-economic phenomenon whose complexity cannot be exhausted by referring to a single economic logic. In this course, Foucault is venturing an interpretation of the history of capitalism no longer dominated by the Marxist logic of capital and its inevitable determinism. Foucault recognizes the unity of capitalism only at the level of economic theory, which is insufficient by itself to understand its different historical figures. He argues that a political interrogation of capitalism needs to set aside the Marxist perspective. It must start from the institutional and economic transformations that determined capitalism's historical reality and predefined its chances of surviving the crises it periodically goes through, all of which cannot be separated from the historical to the singularity to which they belong. Foucault's analysis seeks to satisfy this critical need. First, he discusses liberal governmentality in general terms, then he examines two contemporary versions of it — German and American neoliberalism — as two concrete examples of how liberal governmentality has analyzed and programmed itself.

For Foucault, trying to understand the process of constitution of the market as the locus of veridiction means to problematize the regime of truth that liberalism established. In other words, he wants to highlight how one of the fundamental phenomena of the history of Western modernity conceals the mutual intertwining of jurisdiction and veridiction. In this sense, naturalism much more than liberalism seems to characterize this new art of government.

Freedom, however, is at the heart of this practice of government, which is not content to respect or guarantee this or that freedom but rather "consumes freedom" to the extent that it cannot really function except where some specific freedoms exist: freedom of the market, freedom of the seller and the buyer, free exercise of property, freedom of discussion and expression... "it is clear that at the heart of this liberal practice is an always different and mobile problematic relationship between the production of freedom and that which in the production of freedom risks limiting and destroying it. [. . .] Liberalism must produce freedom, but this very act entails the establishment of limitations, controls, forms of coercion, and obligations relying on threats, etcetera" (Foucault 2010, 64). The liberal art of governing must determine in what exact proportions and within what limits the different individual interests can become a danger to collective interests. It must ensure that the mechanics of the interests are not a source of danger, either to individuals or the community. The relationship between freedom and security is the driving force of this new governing reason, and it presides over a formidable extension of the procedures of control, constraint, and coercion destined to become a sort of counterpart and counterbalance to freedom. We are witnessing the appearance of mechanisms whose function is to produce, inspire, and increase freedom — thereby introducing a surplus of freedom through a surplus of control and intervention.[19]

In Foucault's reading, the main source behind the crises of liberal governmentality is the deep link between liberalism and disciplinary techniques, as well as the paroxysmal increase of mechanisms compensating for freedom.

These crises cannot be considered simply as a direct consequence of the intrinsic crises of capitalist economy's logical development, but rather as crises of the general apparatus of governmentality. Foucault argues that the tendency of all political thought to reduce the concrete and historical multiplicity of the practices of governmentality to the abstract universal of the state conceals the specific nature of these crises. The same hidden universalizing tendency explains why disparate critical approaches eventually converge toward a general phobia of the state that, although always representing a symptom of the governmental crisis, is inherently incapable of providing an adequate diagnosis. In general, the theories that can be traced back to the general theme of *state phobia* exhibit two recurrent *topoi*. First comes the claim that the state's own dynamism gives it a sort of power of expansion and an intrinsic tendency to grow until it takes charge of civil society, which should constitute its other and, at the same time, its target and its object. Second comes the idea of a kinship and even an evolutionary relationship between different forms of state (administrative, welfare, bureaucratic, fascist, totalitarian). These themes put into circulation what Foucault here calls "an inflationary critical mechanism" because they produce interchangeable analyses that lose their specificity. They generate a general devaluation of their critical object. In reality, for Foucault, it is not the increase of the *raison d'État* that is at stake but, on the contrary, its attenuation. In twentieth-century societies, this attenuation becomes apparent in two forms: the decrease of state governmentality through the growth of party governmentality and through liberal governmentality.[20]

For Foucault, the key to understanding the deep mechanisms of liberal governmentality, and, in particular, the freedom-security dialectic that crosses it, is the interrogation of the specific modes of subjectivation that it enacts and upon which it is based. The new governmental reason has two fundamental anchor points: markets and the principle of utility. The former provides an exchange mechanism that functions as the site of veridiction of the relationship between value and price, while the latter limits the intervention of the public authorities (Foucault 2010, 44). We can gather both under a single heading: the new, modern reason for government functions on the basis of interest, which actually consists of a complex mesh of individual and collective interests, social utility, and economic profit: "In its new regime, government is basically no longer to be exercised over subjects and other things subjected through these subjects. Government is now to be exercised over what we could call the phenomenal republic of interests" (Foucault 2010, 46).

In the last lectures of the course, Foucault addresses in detail the problem of the form of subjectivation correlated to the truth regime of liberal and neoliberal governmentality, the *homo œconomicus*: "It also means that the individual becomes governmentalizable, that power gets a hold on him to the extent, and only to the extent, that he is a *homo œconomicus*. That is to say, the surface of contact between the individual and the power exercised on him, and so the principle of the regulation of power over the individual, will be only this kind of grid of *homo œconomicus*. *Homo œconomicus* is the interface of government and the individual" (Foucault 2010, 253). The figure of the *homo oeconomicus* arises at the intersection between the empiricist conception of the subject of interest and the analyses of classical economists. The key point is its total heterogeneity with respect to the subject of law, the related negative logic of contract, and the dialectic of renunciation and transcendence from which law emerges. In fact, in classical and neoclassical economic theory, the *homo oeconomicus* essentially functions as an intangible element with respect to the exercise of power.[21] It is the subject that only obeys its own selfish interest, even though an invisible hand will make it spontaneously converge with the interests of others.[22] The interest-driven *homo oeconomicus* is the only element of intelligibility of necessarily uncontrollable and altogether elusive economic processes. No agent of the economic process must or can strategically seek the collective good and turn it into a goal. The exercise of government must not in any way interfere with that interest; it must obey the rule of laissez-faire. Thus, the world of the economy must necessarily remain substantially obscure even to politics.

Liberalism, in its modern form, starts precisely from the assumption of the incompatibility between the perspective opened up by the elusive multiplicity of subjects of interest and the all-encompassing and unifying instance of sovereign power. This is an important moment because political economy can present itself as a critique of the reason of government since it poses the problem of the impossibility of an economic sovereign. Liberalism offers a sharp contrast to the police state and to the state governed by the *raison d'État*, whose mercantilist policies claimed to administer even the economic processes among individuals in the name of a comprehensive knowledge.

Compared to the classic conception, the neoliberal doctrine of *homo oeconomicus* does not conceive of the individual as a partner in the exchange but rather as an entrepreneur of himself. The individual is the bearer of a human capital composed of innate and acquired elements.[23] From this standpoint, the individual is a *homo oeconomicus* because it is the subject of a behavior that can be interpreted economically. It responds to the variable circumstances it encounters based on the principle of interest and its behavior can be governed through artificial modifications of the environment: "*Homo œconomicus* is someone who is eminently governable. From being the intangible partner of *laissez-faire*, *homo œconomicus* now becomes the correlate of a governmentality which will act on the environment and systematically modify its variables" (Foucault 2010, 270–71). However, *homo oeconomicus* remains irreducible to the sphere of law and therefore is incapable of exhausting the subjective element of the governmental dynamic. Whether it is possible to govern individuals who are both subjects of law and economic actors remains an open question. To avoid splitting itself into two branches, liberal governmentality had to come up with a complex form of subjectivity that would hold together both the economic subject and the subject of law. The answer is civil society: "The problem of civil society is the juridical structure [*économie juridique*] of a governmentality pegged to the economic structure [*économie économique*]" (Foucault 2010, 296).

The Foucauldian problematization of the category of civil society takes its cue, then, precisely from the philosophical-practical horizon of the concept of government. Foucault analyzes civil society as a concept of governmental technology — as a technology necessary to the liberal exercise of government — and not as a historical-natural *datum* nor as a philosophical concept. Therefore, he rejects the dichotomy between civil society and the state as a historical-political universal, providing the starting point for the analysis of concrete systems.

Foucault holds that civil society, like madness and sexuality, is one of the "transactional realities" that arise within the game and relations of power and constantly elude them in the interface between rulers and ruled. Civil society is the concrete whole that gathers individuals conceived as abstract economic actors to balance their abstractness and make them effectively governable. It is a figure that arises precisely from the somehow paradoxical nature of liberal governmentality, a technology of government that has its own self-limitation as a goal. The specific character of liberal governmentality lies in questioning the very necessity of the exercise of government. Since liberal governmentality never presupposes the existence of institutions, contrarily to the rationality of government in terms of *raison d'État*, it can therefore constantly question the usefulness of any institutional intervention. Civil society, which finds itself with respect to the state in a relationship of exteriority and interiority at once, makes it possible to determine the degree of utility/damage of governmental action: "It is the idea of society which permits the development of a technology of government based on the principle that it is already in itself 'too much,' 'excessive' — or at least that it is added as a supplement whose necessity and usefulness can and must always be questioned" (Foucault 2010, 319). On the one hand, *homo oeconomicus* is the ideal correlate of liberalism: it is the bearer of that freedom which must be presupposed but, at the same time, produced and guaranteed by governmental power. On the other hand, civil society is the field of reference of liberal governmentality with respect to its juridical exercise: it is the collective form of subjectivity that must be governed and managed precisely to safeguard the ideal core of individual freedom that must be *left free to act*: "*Homo œconomicus* and civil society are therefore two inseparable elements" (Foucault 2010, 296).

Although Foucault is not explicit on this issue, we may understand the *homo oeconomicus* — civil society combination as a form of subjectivation characteristic of the liberal regime of truth. It presides over a governmentality defined by the freedom-security dialectic, where the proliferation of biopolitical mechanisms and the increase in security and control apparatuses acts as a counterbalance for the principle of self-limitation of government. The biopolitical and security mechanisms correspond, instead, to the form of subjectivation of the population. The population is the object of which the mechanisms of government really take hold. It is for this reason that Foucault affirms that the modern political problem is entirely tied to the population (Foucault 2007b, 105).

On January 25, 1978, Foucault introduced the notion of government for the first time, declaring that "the series, mechanisms of security-population-government and the opening up of the field that we call politics, should be analyzed" (Foucault 2007b, 106). This goal guided him during these two years of lectures. The reason that led Foucault to the analysis of liberalism ultimately turns out to be methodological. Proceeding further along the path he had started to tread the previous year, Foucault wanted to test the very notion of government as a grid of intelligibility of power relations on a concrete historical-political context. He wanted to verify its validity with respect to the entire range of power relations,[24] both those invested by disciplinary power and those at work in biopolitical mechanisms: "What I wanted to do — and this was what was at stake in the analysis — was to see the extent to which we could accept that the analysis of micro-powers, or of procedures of governmentality, is not confined by definition to a precise domain determined by a sector of the scale, but should be considered simply as a point of view, a method of decipherment which may be valid for the whole scale, whatever its size" (Foucault 2010, 186).

3

The Christian Model

Pastoral Care and Government of Truth

I think Foucault's thought is a thought that didn't evolve but went from one crisis to another. I don't believe thinkers can avoid crises, they're too seismic. There's a wonderful remark in Leibniz: "Having established these things, I thought I was coming into port, but when I started to meditate upon the union of the soul with the body, I was as it were thrown back onto the open sea." Indeed, this ability to break the line of thought, to change direction, to find themselves on the open sea, and so discover, invent, is what give thinkers a deeper coherence.

— Deleuze 1995

This chapter focuses on the crisis — the *déplacement* — that, more than any other, threw Foucault back onto the open sea while at the same time allowed him to achieve a higher level of coherence. I am referring to the transition from his previous emphasis on the knowledge-power pair to the new phase that the notion of "government of men by the truth" inaugurates. As I pointed out already, a fundamental characteristic of Foucault's *practical philosophy* is the constant questioning of the conceptual tools and the chosen methods that he follows according to the needs of the analysis and the requirements of the phenomena under scrutiny. Foucauldian philosophy is not *practical* because it applies to a specific field of action a series of theoretical principles developed thanks to a predetermined method. It is thought itself that is *practical* because it is an experience that constitutes itself during its exercise through continuous self-criticism and self-verification.

Indeed, we saw in chapter 2 how the concept of biopolitics emerged in the context of the analysis of disciplinary techniques at the macro-political level and how Foucault then progressively reduced its scope when he focused on its genealogy, eventually bringing it back to the sphere of security devices. The concept of biopolitics, which at first seemed to function as a principle of intelligibility of modern political rationality and as a key to understanding modernity's relations of power, was in fact decentralized and almost undermined by the category of governmentality.

Here it is important to acknowledge the role biopolitics played in the development of the path leading Foucault to the elaboration of the notion of government, via the analysis of pastoral power. In fact, while investigating the phenomena that lead him to the concept of biopower, Foucault's attention turns for the first time to the Christian pastorate, which comes to play an important double role serving, on the one hand, as a model for an alternative analysis of the relations of power that would replace the juridical-repressive power of sovereignty and, on the other hand, as the genealogical matrix of modern power-knowledge devices. In the late 1970s, a close scrutiny of the pastoral model leads Foucault to suggest the concept of government as the key to understanding power relations and as a replacement of the power-knowledge pair.[1] In this chapter, I retrace the key moments of Foucault's analysis of the pastorate, and I show how the focus of his investigations increasingly shifts to the issue of the relationship between the exercise of power and truth manifestations. Finally, I discuss what are the consequences, from the standpoint of Foucault's *practical philosophy*, of the *déplacement* from the power-knowledge pair to the concept of government of truth.

Pastoral Power and People's Government

While working on *The History of Sexuality,* Foucault does not consider Christianity to be a new, fundamentally repressive, form of morality. Rather, he identifies it as the origin of a new mechanism of power and of a series of new power technologies founded on a desire to know. Confession is the most eminent example. Foucault shows how the Christian institution of confession went through remarkable developments since the Middle Ages, starting with the regulation of the sacrament of penance by the Lateran Council of 1215. Eventually, it became the paradigmatic form of authentication of the individual as such. For a long time, confession remained specifically linked to the practice of penance. Yet, little by little, beginning with Protestantism and the Counter-Reformation, and then with eighteenth-century pedagogy and nineteenth-century medicine, confession extends its effects of power to a whole series of other relationships, bringing about a vertiginous increase in the methods of interrogation and inquiry:[2] "The truthful confession was inscribed at the heart of the procedures of individualization by power" (Foucault 1978c, 58–59). The obligation to confess comes from so many different sources that it can no longer be identified as the effect of a coercive power. One gets the impression that it is truth itself that must be revealed through confession and must be freed from the oppression of secrecy: "Confession frees, but power reduces one to silence; truth does not belong to the order of power, but shares an original affinity with freedom:

traditional themes in philosophy, which a 'political history of truth' would have overturned by showing that truth is not by nature free — nor error servile — but that its production is thoroughly imbued with relations of power. The confession is an example of this" (Foucault 1978c, 60). In obeying the obligation of confession, human beings are twice subjugated: they are molded into compliant subjects as well as turned into enunciating subjects who recognize themselves, as individuals, in the act of this very enunciation. The truth that resides in the confession is not guaranteed by the authority of the enunciator nor by a tradition transmitted therein, but rather by the essential belonging of the discourse to the speaker. The authority of the confession comes from the listener's silence, while the effects of the enunciated truth do not affect the listener, but rather the enunciating subject.

First of all, confession is an example of a technology that originates in a productive, rather than repressive, instance of power. In fact, confession produces *identity*. In other words, it is the most apparent manifestation of a mechanism of subjugation that is accomplished through the subjectivation of the individual. The persons who confess bind themselves to identities that, in reality, correspond to the internalized form of a mode of heteronomous subjectivation. Through the mechanism of confession, the individual achieves inner conformity to a determinate regime of truth. Identity, as the internalized form of a heteronomous subjectivation, is the instrument that allows the articulation between the totalizing and individualizing dimensions of a pastoral type of power. This issue emerges clearly in the 1979 to 1980 course at the *Collège de France*, discussed in the next section.

In 1976, Foucault considers the confession, as well as the Christian practices of spiritual direction, as the model of the individualizing technology typical of disciplinary biopower played out against the juridical model of repressive power. With the analysis of the biopolitics of population, it becomes clear how the modern mechanisms of power combine the same individualizing attitude with a totalizing perspective. Starting from the course of 1977 to 1978, as I demonstrated in the previous chapter, Foucault's conceptual research is guided by the search for an organic articulation between the micro- and the macrophysical levels of power. In other words, Foucault seeks to bring to light the articulation between the individualizing and totalizing instances that, in modernity, not only are not opposed but are also intrinsically linked and constitute the core of modern governmentality's security mechanisms. Foucault identifies the matrix of the specific form of the link between these two instances in the *omnes et singulatim* features of Christian pastoral care. In this sense, they are the precursor of the process of governmentalization that marks the specificity of the modern state: "I'd like to underline the fact the state's power (and that's one of the reasons for its strength) is both an individualizing and totalizing form of power. [. . .] This is due to the fact that the modern Western state has integrated in a new political shape, an old power technique which originated in Christian institutions. We can call this power technique the pastoral power" (Foucault

1982, 213). By definition, pastors exercise their power over a flock — on a moving multiplicity — rather than over a territory, like sovereign power. The essential duty of pastors is the salvation of the flock, its constant protection, and daily care first and foremost. It is a power that serves those on whom it is exercised. Shepherds are bound to their flocks by a moral responsibility — it requires their complete dedication and their willingness to sacrifice. Watching over the multiplicity of the flock, however, implies taking charge of every single sheep in the flock. Pastoral power is an individualizing power that is directed to the group — to the totality — only on the condition that no individual escapes its control. Indeed, we could say that the flock as such only exists as the object of the pastor's attention. Therefore, pastoral power is selfless, sacrificial, and individualizing.

The analysis of Christian pastoral ministry as a model of *government* — understood as the specific mode of power that characterizes modernity — engages Foucault for three lectures of the *Security, Territory, Population* course (1977–78) and is repeated on numerous occasions during that same year and the following year.[3] Foucault explains that the idea of a government of men, which was almost completely absent in the Greek and Roman literature, originates in the pre-Christian and later Christian East (Egypt, Assyria, Judea).[4] Characteristics of these early forms are, on the one hand, the idea and organization of a pastoral type of power and, on the other hand, the direction of conscience and souls. The Hebrews are the first to thematize a full and positive form of the pastorate, even though their conception essentially refers to the relationship between God and men.[5] The process that introduced pastoral power in the West is unique in history: this is the process through which a religious community constitutes itself as a Church. The Church is an institution that (1) aspires to govern men in their daily lives under the pretext of leading them to eternal life in another world and (2) directs its pastoral care not to a circumscribed group but to humanity as a whole. The Christian Church codified the theme of the pastorate and gave it absolute autonomy. The model of Christian pastoral gained a central role to produce an identification between religious and pastoral power and to determine the very configuration of the ecclesiastical organization. The Reformation and the Counter-Reformation were a great battle over the exercise of the pastoral office, which neither the Catholic nor the Protestant world were willing to renounce. The specificity of the Christian pastorate lies in the self-generated immense institutional network, which is not found in the Jewish or non-Christian Eastern institutions. The Christian pastorate constructed a true art of leading, directing, and manipulating men, taking charge of them individually and collectively throughout their existence: "It is an art of 'governing men,' and I think this is where we should look for the origin, the point of formation, of crystallization, the embryonic point of the governmentality whose entry into politics, at the end of the sixteenth and in the seventeenth and eighteenth centuries, marks the threshold of the modern state. The modern state is born, I think, when governmentality became a calculated and reflected practice" (Foucault 2007b, 222). Foucault's analysis identifies salvation, law, and truth as the three elements constituting the specific deep structure of Christian pastoral ministry: " . . . the pastor guides to salvation, prescribes the law, and teaches the truth" (Foucault 2007b, 224). These three themes are central to both the fundamental dynamics of the Christian pastorate (directing consciences and leading conducts), and to the Christian transformation of Jewish pastorate. In turn, the secularization of these three elements, Foucault argues, constitutes modern governmentality. The task of the pastors is to make people advance on the path to salvation. They must secure the salvation of the community as a whole and of each of its members. With Christianity, shepherds' responsibilities for the destiny of their flocks also extend to all individual actions of each sheep. A very close moral bond binds Christian shepherds to each one of the faithful: they are responsible for the sins of each and every one, and their own salvation is subordinate to the salvation of the flock for which they care. At the same time, salvation is a duty that leaves the individual no freedom of choice: "The power of the pastor consists precisely in that he has the authority to require the people to do everything necessary for their salvation: obligatory salvation" (Foucault 1999b, 124).

Second, the pastor must make the law and the will of God known. The most characteristic feature of this second theme, however, is the relationship of integral dependence and submission binding the sheep to the shepherd. To be obeyed is not the law itself, it is rather the will of the shepherd as it emerges in the individual relationship with the sheep. The Christian pastorate inaugurates *pure obedience*, a form of obedience without any rational mediation, nor any goal other than obedience itself. Its practice, humility, is considered a virtue, and it is characterized by the final renunciation and mortification of all autonomous will: "pastoral power [. . .] not only does not take place by way of affirmation of the self, but [. . .] entails destruction of the self" (Foucault 2007b, 235–36).

Finally, a twofold constraint links salvation to truth in the Christian pastorate. On the one hand, there is a truth that must be believed and professed by the faithful individuals. The pastor must teach this truth, which constitutes the basis for absolute obedience. The first task of the pastor towards the community is, therefore, teaching. On the other hand, there is a truth that must be produced by the faithful, so the pastor can guide their conduct and direct their conscience. The pastor's teaching task is not limited to the transmission of a theoretical truth content — it must become direction of conduct and direction of conscience. Both practices compel the shepherd to know the sheep and take charge of their daily conduct through observation and comprehensive analytical supervision. Contrary to ancient practices, the Christian direction of conscience is by no means voluntary, circumstantial, or aimed at the individual's self-mastery. It is an instrument of individualization that seeks a continuous and permanent dependence. Its goal is the manifestation of unconditional obedience through the production of a specific secret truth of the soul. Its aim is a form of subjugation that requires a generalized servitude and the verbalization of an internal hidden truth. The greatest transformation wrought by Christian pastoral care with respect to its Jewish counterpart lies precisely in having introduced a whole series of techniques of examination and confession — manifestations of obedience aiming at mortification and the renunciation of the relationship of self with self and the world.

The deeper analyses of the relationship between power-truth or, rather, government-truth — starting from the analysis of the techniques of subjectivation that the Christian model introduced in the West — are a particularly important moment in the journey that concludes Foucault's 1970s research and, at the same time, paves the way for those studies that will engage him in his last years.

Governing Truth

The important role that Foucault's analysis of Christian pastorate plays with respect to his genealogy of modern governmentality goes beyond the emphasis on the simultaneously individualizing and totalizing features of pastoral power. At the beginning of the 1980s, this analysis becomes a pivot that marks a particularly significant transition in his philosophical path.

In the 1979 to 1980 course at the *Collège de France* titled *On the Government of the Living* and in the American conferences of the following fall, Foucault centers the genealogical analysis of the Christian model on the self-reflective truth-practices that have the individual as both subject and object. In is in this context that the structure of reciprocal implications tying together the three problems regarded by Foucault as the three main axes of his research — the problem of truth, the problem of power, and the problem of individuals' relationship with themselves[6] — explicitly emerges for the first time.

First, with this course Foucault concludes his long inquiry into modernity, its specific relations of power, and its modalities of individuals' subjectivation. As we saw in the previous chapter, Foucault had started — not culminated, as Dreyfus and Rabinow's interpretation would posit — such an investigation in 1976 with the introduction of the concept of biopower. It was an attempt to organize the particular and dispersed research projects of the early 1970s within a broader philosophical perspective. Therefore, it does not seem to be a coincidence that the title of the course simultaneously refers to the *biological* dimension and to the notion of *government* that had served as the conceptual keystones of Foucault's entire reflection. Secondly, rather than merely providing the conclusion of a path, this course offers a very productive transition and a springboard into the next phase of Foucault's research. Yet the next section in this chapter reviews in more detail why it is a mistake to interpret this particular stage of Foucault's thought as a turning point.

The course dedicated to the "government of the living" opens in a quite unusual way for Foucault with a universal and assertive theoretical suggestion. This is the idea that the exercise of power is always accompanied by a manifestation of a "non-economic," apparently self-contained truth supplementing the set of systematically organized pieces of knowledge that the exercise of government requires. Foucault suggests that directing people entails the recourse to certain operations of truth that exceed what is needed to govern effectively. It is necessary to engage in a purely ritual manifestation of truth that exceeds governmental reason and the rational art of governing with which Foucault dealt in previous years. Foucault proposes the term *alethurgy* for such a manifestation of truth:

> We could call "alethurgy" the manifestation of truth as the set of possible verbal or non-verbal procedures by which one brings to light what is laid down as true as opposed to false, hidden, inexpressible, unforeseeable, or forgotten, and say that there is no exercise of power without something like an alethurgy. Or again — since you know that I love Greek words and that in Greek the exercise of power is called "hegemony," although not in the sense we now give this word: hegemony is just the fact of being in the position of leading others, of conducting them, and of conducting, as it were, their conduct — I will say: it is likely that hegemony cannot be exercised without something like an alethurgy. (Foucault 2016b, 7)[7]

Foucault does not analytically develop the intrinsic connection between *alethurgy* and power, nor does he really thematize it. Rather, he presents it ostensively through the example of the emperor Septimius Severus, which opens the course, and through the analysis of Sophocles's *Oedipus Rex*, to which the second and third lectures are entirely devoted.[8] This is because, at this juncture, this idea is essentially a tool, serving to connect and, at the same time, clarify the research carried out in previous years. Indeed, Foucault emphasizes that he cannot consider the genealogical investigation of governmentality to be concluded, but, on the contrary, it is necessary to broaden its scope to question the specific *alethurgical* form accompanying such a mode of governing. The example of Oedipus, in particular, allows Foucault to introduce the issue of subjectivation through the reflexive manifestation of truth — that is, its *alethurgical* mode — that characterizes modern governmentality: "Why, in what form, in a society like ours, is there such a deep bond between the exercise of power and the obligation for individuals to become themselves essential actors in the procedures of manifestation of the truth, in the procedures of alethurgy needed by power? What is the relationship between the fact of being subject in a relation of power and a subject through which, for which, and regarding which the truth is manifested?" (Foucault 2016b, 80–81). Foucault answers with the usual anarcho-genealogical research, which once again resorts to the Christian model and its secularization. Christianity is a religion characterized by a double regime of truth: a "regime of faith" and a "regime of confession." The former imposes so-called acts of faith upon the Christian: the acceptance of a revealed content; the obligation to hold as true several dogmas and accept specific books as sources of truth; the assent to the decisions on truth that have been issued by determinate authorities. On the other hand, the second truth regime imposes reflected acts of truth (i.e., alethurgical procedures) in which the individual is simultaneously operator, spectator/witness, and object. The confession of sins represents a paradigmatic example of such acts.

After treating the theme of Christian pastoral care and confession in general terms, Foucault begins to investigate in detail the origins of the obligation to perform acts of truth. In particular, he is interested in the pre-baptismal rites of purification and penance in early Christianity and in the practice of the direction of conscience in the monastic context, before penance was organized as a sacrament (twelfth to thirteenth century).[9] Foucault focuses on the Church fathers' conception of the path to salvation in relation to truth, and on the kind of practices and rituals prescribed to early Christians who were pursuing such a path.

The course's overall goal is to offer a history of the practices of truth that see subjects turning to themselves and making themselves objects not simply of knowledge but also of transformation. On the one hand, this general stance is motivated by the need to stress the specificity of the Christian link between confession, conversion, error, and salvation. On the other hand, it follows from Foucault's intention to examine whether the technologies of the self may result in an active and autonomous construction of subjectivity that could provide a possible resistance against subjectivation processes. In other words, the course intends both to conclude Foucault's research of recent years with a critical and detailed analysis of the Christian techniques of subjectivation as a matrix of their modern counterpart and, at the same time, to prepare the ground for the problems that future courses address. Foucault wants to show how the Christian techniques of the hermeneutics of the self constitutes the model for the human sciences' goal of an infinite work of interpretation of the self. Foucault's *practical philosophy* clearly aims to distance itself from such a goal:

> But the moment, maybe, is coming for us to ask, do we need, really, this hermeneutics of the self? Maybe the problem of the self is not to discover what it is in its positivity, maybe the problem is not to discover positive self or the positive foundation of the self. Maybe our problem is now to discover that the self is nothing other than the historical correlation of the technology built in our history. Maybe the problem is to change those technologies. And in this case, one of the main political problems would be nowadays, in the strict sense of the word, the politics of ourselves. (Foucault 2016a, 76)

The key passages of the last part of the course devoted to a genealogy of confession within the history of Christianity are worth reporting. According to Foucault, the specificity of Christian confessional practice, in particular regarding the direction and examination of conscience in the Stoic and Epicurean traditions, arises from the tension between a system of salvation and a system of law within Christianity. Since the system of law addresses individuals' single actions distinguishing between good and evil, conforming and non-conforming, the succession from error to sanction is indefinitely replicable. The system of salvation, however, addresses an individual's quality of life by partitioning it in two parts based on the unique and irreversible event of conversion. The novelty of Christianity, with respect to both Judaism and Greek culture, lies in the attempt to reconcile these two irreconcilable systems through the idea of the relapse (*rechute*) into error and sin, and the related possibility of renewing the act of conversion. Between the third and seventh centuries AD, the problem of the repeatability of conversion and penance underwent a rather complex doctrinal and liturgical evolution. The Christian practice of confession emerged in this context. Initially, penance was not an act but rather a long-term status that prevented the sinner from facing a definitive expulsion from the community.[10] Penance was characterized by obligations and prohibitions, some of which remained in place after forgiveness was granted.[11] The penitent is subjected to a number of truth procedures. Some are objective, in which case members of the community are its operators, and some are reflexive, in which case the penitents themselves become the operators of the manifestation of truth. In this course, Foucault is clearly more interested in the reflexive operations of truth, even though there is a clear connection with his previous research on the penal and psychiatric systems.[12]

The term *exomologesis*, sometimes translated by Latin commentators with the expression *publicatio sui*, refers to the penitents' reflective truth obligations. Sometimes, the term designates only the episode of dramatically pleading self-expression that the penitents must face when they are being reinstated. More frequently, it identifies the whole complex of acts that must be carry out by the penitent to obtain reconciliation. In *exomologesis* the punishment for one's sins is inseparable from a voluntary self-manifestation, and it coincides with a theatricalization of the very condition of being a penitent that passes through the body. The baseness of sin is publicly exposed and sin itself is represented, in a dramatic scene of self-denial and self-destruction, as an allegory of death. The penitents must show themselves as having renounced the purity and splendor of the faith for the misery and filth of corruption and sin.[13] In this stage, the true verbal presentation of sin, its enunciation, is not yet part of the penitential procedure, but precedes it. The *confessio* happens when the sinners present their case in order to ask that they be granted the status of penitent. It is only from the twelfth century forward that the presentation of the case becomes part of the penitential process and replaces the *publicatio sui*. From this moment onward, the relationship between the subject and truth is codified under the law and filtered through a discursive practice. It is only then that Christian penance receives its present form and creates the basis of Western subjectivity's particular relationship with discourse and confession:

> [I think that] the appearance of these two procedures, first, the detailed verbalization of the sin by the subject who committed it and, second, the procedures of knowledge, discovery, and exploration of oneself, and the coupling of these two procedures, that of the detailed verbalization of the sin and that of the exploration of oneself, is an important phenomenon, [the] appearance [of which] in Christianity and, generally, in the Western world, marks, I believe, the beginning of an ultimately very lengthy process in which the subjectivity of Western man is developed — and by subjectivity I understand the mode of relation of self to self. (Foucault 2016b, 225)

In fact, says Foucault, such a coupling of self-exploration and verbalization of error first appears in the fourth century, when monasticism recovers and radically transforms the techniques of examination and direction of conscience that flourished in late classical philosophy. Obedience and contemplation are the two fundamental principles marking the exercise of confession in monastic communities. Obedience is a permanent and unconditional obligation: the monks must always preserve the spirit of obedience as a perpetual sacrifice of their own will and their own selves, even when they become teachers. The contemplation of God is the ultimate goal. This is why the Christian examination of conscience addresses more so the flow of thoughts that can distract attention from God rather than the performed acts. Introspection is not targeting the passions that may compromise a monk's righteous behavior, but rather the imperceptible movements of the soul that may interfere with contemplation. To be able to keep their gaze constantly fixed on God, the monks must examine every idea because their purity and authenticity do not depend on their possible correspondence to external reality but rather depend on the divine, non-demonic inspiration from which they originated. Such a difficult hermeneutic work requires confession to the spiritual father: on the one hand, because the teacher's seniority allows him to better distinguish between truth and illusion, and on the other, because the verbal act of confession allows the monk to interpret and test the goodness of the thoughts through a performative act of exposure to the divine eyes of the mind's inner motion. The Greek fathers called such a monastic practice of verbalizing thoughts *exagoreusis*.

Foucault's analysis of the two Christian truth practices of *exomologesis* and *exagoreusis* seeks, above all, to emphasize their profound connection. The former acts through the mortification of the body, while the latter acts through the obligation to the permanent enunciation of thoughts. Both practices express the same Christian principle, according to which the revelation of the truth about oneself is not dissociable from one's own self-denial in obedience.

Foucault argues that obedience is both the founding principle and the final goal of the Christian technologies of subjectivation. Christian obedience has no other end than itself; its aim is to produce a state of obedience. It is a form of obedience that concerns the subject's relationship with others and to the events of the external world just as much as it concerns the disposition of the individual's own will. Christian obedience takes the form of submission, patience, and humility. It demands submission to the will of the other; it prescribes patience as an attitude toward the external world that requires a passive and inert tolerance of events; it exacts humility in the relationship with oneself by disqualifying one's own will and placing oneself in a position that is as inferior and subordinate to others as possible.

The fundamental instrument that guarantees this obedience is precisely the perpetual and exhaustive confession of oneself, the constant verbalization of the incessant self-examination: the characteristic form of Christian subjectivation is the reciprocal implication between the production of one's own truth and self-denial. Obviously, this form of subjectivation would be unthinkable if it were not embedded in a system of power relations and subjected to an individualizing and totalizing power whose exercise, in turn, implies such an infinite obligation of truth — namely, pastoral power. In making the practices of reflected truth an instrument of obedience, and in transforming the technologies of the self — which in antiquity were the preferred path toward the achievement of autonomous subjectivation — into technologies of domination, Christianity short-circuits and newly articulates the analytical and globalizing dimensions of pastoral power.

If modern governmentality originates in the secularization of the pastoral *omnes et singulatim* model, it is clear that it must also imply the hermeneutics of the individual as one of its components. In the governmental context, the hermeneutics of the individual as an instrument of subjectivation is detached from doctrine and grounded on empirical anthropological knowledge. It becomes the goal of judicial and psychiatric institutions, medical and psychoanalytic practices, and the so-called human sciences: "In addition, human sciences are knowledges that allow the recognition of what individuals are, who is capable, and to do what, what are individuals' predictable behaviors, who are those one has to eliminate" (Foucault 1978d, 199).

Modern governmentality repeats the twofold relationship with the truth characteristic of pastoral power in its secular context: the pedagogical relationship with doctrine and the hermeneutical relationship with the confession of sins reappear, respectively, under the guise of the human sciences and as individual confessions in the most diverse contexts.

In this sense, as Foucault had said in 1976 already,

> The confession has spread its effects far and wide. It plays a part in justice, medicine, education, family relationships, and

> love relations, in the most ordinary affairs of everyday life, and in the most solemn rites; one confesses one's crimes, one's sins, one's thoughts and desires, one's illnesses and troubles; one goes about telling, with the greatest precision, whatever is most difficult to tell. One confesses in public and in private, to one's parents, one's educators, one's doctor, to those one loves; one admits to oneself, in pleasure and in pain, things it would be impossible to tell to anyone else, the things people write books about. One confesses — or is forced to confess. [...] Western man has become a confessing animal. (Foucault 2013b, 59)

Why the Concept of "Government"

In the previous section, we saw how the discussion of the government of truth concludes the path Foucault started in 1978 with *Security, Territory, Population*. The concept of governmentality relegates the idea of biopolitics to a completely secondary role, and it gains a central role in his thought as the principle of intelligibility of modernity's power relations. In the 1979 to 1980 course, the issue of the government of truth emerges as a transition, rather than a *turning point*, and it settles the overall conceptual coordinates and prepares the ground for the problems that will engage Foucault in the following years: self-care and the practices of active subjectivation of individuals, on the one hand, *parrhēsia* and the role of the philosopher, on the other.

With the elaboration of the notion of government of men by the truth, Foucault distanced himself from the power-knowledge pair that had accompanied him throughout the previous decade. In the 1978 course, the comparison with the Christian model offers Foucault the chance to assess the potential of the notion of government and put it to the test. In the first instance, Foucault uses the concept of government to define the specific characteristics of the modern configuration of power-knowledge relations in terms of governmentality and governmentalization. Second, as he traces back to the model of the Christian pastorate the genealogy of this particular mode of power that has in individual practices of truth its pivotal technology, Foucault seems to realize that — with respect to the general outlook of his philosophical journey — governmentality offers a series of significant speculative advantages that go beyond the interpretation of modernity.

In fact, it turns out that the idea of government offers to Foucault's general *practical philosophy* an extremely fruitful tool that makes it possible to analyze the historical-practical constitution of subjectivity in relation to specific regimes and practices of truth, as well as the matrix of power relations in which it is inserted. It also enables the identification of possibilities of resistance and the active exercise of freedom:

> I think that if one wants to analyze the genealogy of the subject in Western civilization, he has to take into account not only techniques of domination but also techniques of the self. [...] He has to take into account the points where the technologies of domination of individuals over one another have recourse to processes by which the individual acts upon himself. And conversely, he has to take into account the points where the techniques of the self are integrated into structures of coercion or domination. The contact point, where the way individuals are driven by others is tied to the way they conduct themselves, is what we can call, I think, government. (Foucault 2016a, 25–26)

As this passage clearly states, Foucault sees the fruitfulness of the concept of government in providing a "contact point," a connecting element.

In the context of Foucault's thought, the concept of government immediately acquires a much broader scope than its current meaning of "the supreme instance of executive and administrative decisions in State systems" (Foucault 2016b, 12). Foucault always wanted to use the term *government* to refer to a set of techniques and procedures designed to guide people's *conduct*: to govern means to steer someone's behavior through different possible actions depending on their various consequences. The fundamental ambiguity of the word *conduct* provides an important clue to a proper understanding of Foucault's choice of the term *government*. The meaning of *conduct*, in fact, simultaneously refers to a heteronormative (or even coercive) instance of behavior and to an individual *ēthos*, a form of behavior more or less autonomously chosen from a field of possibilities. Thus, the function of guidance — which *government* alludes to — does not necessarily coincide with domination, and it coincides even less so with the exercise of a political, juridical, or administrative power. On the contrary, it can also refer to individuals' active production of their own subjectivity. The government of men is articulated through the delicate and versatile balance between how individuals are guided by others and how they act on themselves, between coercion and construction of the self. As we will see more fully in the next chapter, even the individual *ēthos-poietic* exercise of self-care involves technologies in which the other, understood precisely as a guide, plays an essential role. Understood this way, the notion of *government* effectively fulfills Foucault's need to think of power as a mode of action that seeks to guide, direct, and influence the actions of others and that is always already in place in the relationships among free subjects. At the same time, it brings forth the need to rethink subjectivity as a practical subjectivity constituted through the relationship of self to self that exercises freedom through an active resistance requiring, first and foremost, its own autonomous re-subjectivation:

> In other words, what I mean is this: if we take the question of power, of political power, situating it in the more general question of governmentality understood as a strategic field of power relations in the broadest and not merely political sense

> of the term, if we understand by governmentality a strategic field of power relations in their mobility, transformability, and reversibility, then I do not think that reflection on this notion of governmentality can avoid passing through, theoretically and practically, the element of a subject defined by the relationship of self to self. Although the theory of political power as an institution usually refers to a juridical conception of the subject of right, it seems to me that the analysis of governmentality — that is to say, of power as a set of reversible relationships — must refer to an ethics of the subject defined by the relationship of self to self. (Foucault 2005, 252)

Thus, paradoxically, the term *government* ends up undermining power by defining the specificity of power relations. This happens precisely because of the breadth and the particular implications of the semantic field of the concept of government, which may possibly refer to both the techniques of coercion and the techniques of the self, and to both the globalizing power focused on collective subjects such as populations and the analytical molecular power targeting individuals. Overall, the flexibility of the notion of government offers a broader perspective that can account for the multiple potential ways the inherent scattered techniques pertaining to different modes of power can be historically articulated and transform one another.

With the development of the power-knowledge pair, Foucault meant to go beyond the Marxist notion of dominant ideology, which as we saw, he essentially considered to be an incomplete theory of representation that remains trapped into the typical impasses of the subjectivist perspective and is, therefore, unable to provide an account of the real mechanisms of subjugation and subjectivation. And yet, Foucault points out that the very notion of knowledge-power required a further shift — a *déplacement* — that is, a passage to the notion of "government of men by the truth":

> Now, the second shift in relation to this notion of knowledge-power involves getting rid of this in order to try to develop the notion of government by the truth; getting rid of the notion of knowledge-power as we got rid of the notion of dominant ideology. Well, when I say this I am being utterly hypocritical, since it is obvious that one does not get rid of what one has thought oneself in the same way as one rids oneself of what was thought by others. Consequently, I will certainly be more indulgent with the notion of knowledge-power than with that of dominant ideology, but it is for you to reproach me for this. So, in the inability to treat myself as I have treated others, I will say that passing from the notion of knowledge-power to that of government by the truth essentially involves giving a positive and differentiated content to these two terms of knowledge and power. (Foucault 2016b, 12)

We saw how the concept of *government* allows us to "give a positive and differentiated content" to the term *power*. Thus, it is now a matter of understanding in what sense the concept of truth proposed by Foucault in this course gives a positive and differentiated content to the term *knowledge*. In other words, we need to understand what Foucault means when he wishes "to develop the notion of knowledge in the direction of the problem of the truth," according to what he says in the first introductory lecture of *On the Government of the Living* (Foucault 2016b, 12).

The characteristic move of Foucault's *practical philosophy* is to critically reverse the traditional mode of analysis that presupposes a universal subject and a universal truth as given foundations. Foucault does not intend to pose the philosophical-political problem of government from a precise, voluntarily acquired truth, nor to examine a given representation as true or false to determine the legitimacy of power. Thus, it is not a matter of contrasting a self-styled scientific theory to an ideological tale.[14] Rather, Foucault seeks to bring into question the relationship of the subject to truth. This means striving to understand it as historically determined, starting with questioning the specific mechanisms of government that have organized it, in order to show how it is possible to transform this relationship and how, from this transformation, something like resistance is possible. By showing how specific practices of truth are necessary for the exercise of the government of people's conduct, Foucault thus clears the path to the next phase of his research — namely, the phase that deals with the possibility of transformative and emancipatory practices of truth, and with the possibility of active exercise of autonomous subjectivation through self-care or, if you will, self-governance, as a form of resistance.

In the 1979 to 1980 course, Foucault showed how reflexive acts of truth form part of what he calls "regimes of truth." They are procedures and institutions that bind subjects to determinate contents and criteria of truth and force them to perform specific acts of truth. On the one hand, these regimes of truth make the government of men possible, because they provide the normative context in which subjectivity is constituted. On the other hand, they control and consolidate the effects of government through the constitution of individuals' subjectivity as identitarian forms. Foucault argues that this is the only standpoint allowing one to ask how the processes of subjectivation can escape the normative frameworks the regimes of truth set up. Only from this standpoint does it become possible to ask in what sense a critical examination of these regimes of truth may represent an essential mode of resistance and a precondition of any practice of freedom understood as autonomous *ēthopoiesis*. Only from this standpoint can one inquire in what sense a practice of truth, such as the Greek *parrhēsia*, is to be understood as a *conditio sine qua non* of any process of autonomous subjectivation and, at the same time, as the task of the philosopher — not to say its exclusive prerogative.

It is clear, then, that Foucault's *déplacement* from the power-knowledge pair to the concept of "government by the truth" is far from representing a turning point that would have led him to an ethical and intimist retreat. On the contrary, it is a shift, a conceptual adjustment entirely consistent with the general stance, which I have tried to define with the expression *practical philosophy* and is necessary to its further development. A development that, as we shall see, clearly goes in the direction of safeguarding the possibility of thinking freedom in a strong sense. The next chapter is, therefore, entirely devoted to the elucidation of these issues at the center of the last phase of Foucault's thought. Given that such issues are also the endpoints of Michel Foucault's path, they make it possible to venture a critical appraisal of his overall philosophical proposal.

4
Subjectivation Processes and the Task of Philosophy

Not the Greeks, but our relation to subjectivation, our ways of constituting ourselves as subjects. Thinking is always experiencing, experimenting, not interpreting but experimenting, and what we experience, experiment with, is always actuality, what's coming into being, what's new, what's taking shape. History isn't experimentation, it's only the set of conditions, negative conditions almost, that make it possible to experience, experiment with, something beyond history. Without history the experiments would remain indeterminate, divorced from any particular conditions, but the experimentation itself is philosophical rather than historical.

— Deleuze 1995[1]

The previous chapter emphasized the importance of the *déplacement* that occurs in Foucault's analysis as he moves from his earlier power-knowledge horizon to the concept of government of truth. First of all, this shift allows Foucault to account for the internal articulation of the simultaneously individualizing and totalizing mechanisms of power that characterize modern governmentality. Second, the concept of *government of truth* bridges the technologies of domination with the techniques of the self, connecting the inquiries about power mechanisms with one regarding the possibility of individuals' freedom. Thus, it clears the path for a transition from questioning subjugation processes to investigating the possibilities of individual autonomous subjectivation.

In other words, the *government of truth* opens an inquiry about how subjectivation processes may exceed the intertwining relations of power and knowledge whose analysis was Foucault's main concern until the end of the 1970s. This transition — which has been mistakenly characterized as a "turning point" — is therefore to be understood neither as an ethical retreat nor as a return to the subject. Rather, it is a further step toward a radicalization of Foucault's thought in the direction of *practical philosophy*: "He was reorienting all his research in terms of what he called modes of subjectivation. It was nothing to do with returning to the subject, he was creating something new, breaking out along a new line, a new exploration no longer concerned with knowledge and power in the same way. Another radicalization, if you like" (Deleuze 1995, 105). Thematizing such a surplus of subjectivation processes, Foucault inaugurates the *an-archaeo-genealogical* investigation around the third axis of experience that constitutes subjectivity: individuals' relationship with themselves. Deleuze is very clear when he says that Foucault discovers the relation to self "as a new dimension that cannot be reduced to the power-relations and relations between forms of knowledge that were the object of previous books: the whole system has to be reorganized" (Deleuze 1988, 101). After the concept of *government of truth* made this transition possible, Foucault succeeds in reorganizing into a single framework the interweaving of connections that link together what he considers as the three main axes of every experience: "the forms of a possible knowledge," "the normative matrices of individual behavior" and finally "the virtual modes of existence of possible subjects."

At the outset, Foucault devotes himself to the study of one of the three dimensions. Even though he focuses, in each case, on a determinate historical context of experience (the human sciences, madness, disease, criminality, sexuality), he always tries to refer each of them back to the other two dimensions and move from the traditional conception to *practical philosophy*. Foucault's first line of inquiry[2] concerned the formation of knowledge. He studies experience as a matrix for the formation of knowledge and focuses on the discursive practices that, as forms of veridiction, organize it. Then,[3] Foucault turns to the analysis of the normative matrices of behavior and the techniques and procedures that direct the conduct of others. Finally, in a third and final line of inquiry[4] briefly discussed in the next section, Foucault analyzes the constitution of the subject's mode of being and the different forms through which individuals have come to constitute themselves as subjects: "Replacing the history of knowledge with the historical analysis of forms of veridiction, replacing the history of domination with the historical analysis of procedures of governmentality, and replacing the theory of the subject or the history of subjectivity with the historical analysis of the pragmatics of self and the forms it has taken, are the different approaches by which I have tried to define to some degree the possibility of the history of what could be called 'experiences.'"[5] This third line of inquiry leads Foucault to extend his genealogical analysis to Greco-Roman antiquity, whose ethics offer him the means and materials to deepen his reflection on the issue of subjectivation through the relationship of self with self. Moreover, reflecting on the forms that the *government of truth* assumed in antiquity, Foucault has the chance to focus and reorganize the entire complex articulation of cross-references between the three dimensions of the subject's space of constitution — that is, the three dimensions of *praxis* in the broad sense that I have used since the first chapter. Indeed, as I show in this chapter, it is within this framework that one understands Foucault's interest in the Greek concept of *parrhēsia*, which he approached for the first time during the 1981 to 1982 course *The*

Hermeneutics of the Subject and to which he devoted his last two courses at the *Collège de France*: *The Government of Self and Others* (1982–1983) and *The Courage of Truth* (1983–1984).

Through the discussion on the Greek concept of *parrhēsia*, Foucault considers the role of alterity in the processes of subjectivation, and the related issue of the role of the philosopher in relation to politics. In the courses of his last few years, the study of *parrhēsia* and a repeated confrontation with the Kantian question *Was ist Aufklärung?* [*What Is Enlightenment?*] allow Foucault to leverage the potentialities of the notion of *government of truth* and to bring to the fore a discussion of the task of philosophy, an issue that had always been present yet left in the background. This is the theme of the last section of this chapter.

Autonomous Subjectivation and the Care of the Self

In a 1982 interview, Foucault tried to explain the latest developments in his research as follows:

> I do not believe that the only possible point of resistance to political power — understood, of course, as a state of domination — lies in the relationship of the self to the self. I am saying that "governmentality" implies the relationship of the self to itself, and I intend this concept of "governmentality" to cover the whole range of practices that constitute, define, organize, and instrumentalize the strategies that individuals in their freedom can use in dealing with each other. Those who try to control, determine, and limit the freedom of others are themselves free individuals who have at their disposal certain instruments they can use to govern others. Thus, the basis for all this is freedom, the relationship of the self to itself and the relationship to the other. Whereas, if you try to analyze power not on the basis of freedom, strategies, and governmentality, but on the basis of the political institution, you can only conceive of the subject as a subject of law. One then has a subject who has or does not have rights, who has had these rights either granted or removed by the institution of political society; and all this brings us back to a legal concept of the subject. On the other hand, I believe that the concept of governmentality makes it possible to bring out the freedom of the subject and its relationship to others — which constitutes the very stuff [*matière*] of ethics. (Foucault 1997a, 299–300)

Thus, the subject's freedom comes to the fore when Foucault shifts his attention from the government of others to the government of the self. Within the horizon of Foucault's *practical philosophy*, the issue of freedom becomes the issue of the practice of freedom considered as it actually takes place. Since subjectivity is practically constituted and it is not an abstract and universal entity, its freedom cannot be conceived as an abstract and universal attribute. After distancing oneself from the juridical theory of the subject, one cannot conceive freedom in juridical terms. If subjectivity is thought of as the product of relationships among ever mobile individuals who are historically determined by the regime of truth to which they belong, then a subject's freedom is the freedom of subjectivation. Freedom is the subjects' possibility to autonomously constitute themselves and resist domination — that is to say, to resist those asymmetrical relations of power strategically aimed at the subjection of others and at limiting the margins of this very freedom of subjectivation (Foucault 1997a, 291–93). In this sense, the question about freedom is the question about the active role of the individual in the processes of subjectivation. This is the ethical question par excellence.

When Foucault begins his confrontation with ancient ethics in the 1979 to 1980 course, he does so indirectly and in a subdued way following the steps of the genealogy of the hermeneutics of the self in the Christian world that he had traced earlier (see chapter 3). Initially, Foucault is mainly looking for a touchstone: essentially, late antiquity's technologies of government of self are called upon to counterbalance Christianity's techniques of government of truth. In particular, Foucault lingers on the comparison between the opposing ways of understanding the practices of direction and examination of conscience in order to convey the extent of the novelty introduced by Christianity in spite of its origin. Christian pastoral care implies absolute and permanent obedience, unconditional submission, and renunciation of one's own will in view of a salvation that is presented as obligatory. In the Stoic and Epicurean direction of conscience there is no renouncing of the will or the sovereignty over oneself. A free, voluntary, and provisional submission to the master is instrumental to a learning process based on persuasion. Its ultimate, totally immanent purpose is the conquest of a different relationship with oneself and a determinate form of subjectivation.

This brief incursion into antiquity offers Foucault the possibility to open a direct and twofold confrontation with ancient ethics. First, he intends to complete the *an-archaeo-genealogical* research aimed at the problematization of the forms of modern subjectivation to reveal them as being historical and contingent, rather than natural and necessary. Second, ancient ethics provides a ground for an inquiry into the question of freedom and the modes of autonomous subjectivation.

While clarifying Foucault's interest in antiquity, Deleuze explains that the great novelty of the Greeks appears thanks to a double "separation" because,

> the "exercises that enabled one to govern oneself" become detached both from power as a relation between forces, and

> from knowledge as a stratified form, or "code" of virtue. On the one hand there is a "relation to oneself" that consciously derives from one's relation with others; on the other there is equally a "self-constitution" that consciously derives from the moral code as a rule for knowledge. This derivative or differentiation must be understood in the sense in which the relation to oneself assumes an independent status. (Deleuze 1988, 100)

Foucault explicitly thematizes Greek ethics and the ancient practices of government of the self in the 1980 to 1981 course, *Subjectivity and Truth*, and in the course of 1981 to 1982, *The Hermeneutics of the Subject*. They are the laboratory from which the last two volumes of *The History of Sexuality* were born. The first course discusses the issue in relation to the problem of the regime of sexual behavior and sexual pleasures in antiquity, while the second course presents it in more general terms. However, both courses confront their subject matter from essentially the same standpoint: Foucault analyzes Greek ethics as a historical form of the relationship between subjectivity and truth, which cannot be traced back to the typical model of hermeneutics of the self that modernity has inherited from Christianity and that he had discussed in the 1980 course. In other words, it is a matter of moving to a different outlook on the techniques of the self in subjectivation processes and considering the issue of the government of the self from a standpoint other than the pastoral model as well as it is imperative to know and verbalize a certain truth of the self. This is the standpoint of the *care of the self*.

The *care of the self* is the Platonic imperative of the *epimeleia heautou* that, Foucault suggests, is the general frame of reference of ancient ethics. Clearly, Foucault is not after a trivial comparison between different codes of behavior. Rather, he intends to interrogate two different ways to reflect on the individuals' freedom of subjectivation, on the individuals' possibilities to establish a relationship with themselves as acting subjects, and on the practices that must support these actions. This is a chance to reflect on the conduct of the individual as a mode of subjectivation: "I think that the great changes which occurred between Greek society, Greek ethics, Greek morality and how the Christians viewed themselves are not in the code, but in what I call the 'ethics,' which is the relation to oneself" (Dreyfus and Rabinow 1982, 240). Indeed, Foucault (1990, 2:25–32) insists that the common understanding of "morality" actually involves two constitutive aspects: the behavioral code of conduct is the normative component, while the forms of subjectivation and the practices through which subjects constitute themselves as "moral" subjects constitutes its ethical counterpart. It seems clear, therefore, that the comparison between Christian and ancient morality also involves a comparison between a "morality" that emphasizes prescriptions and codes of conduct — that is to say, a normative morality whose subjectivation mode is fundamentally juridical — and a morality that insists on the form of subjectivation, on the *ēthos,* and on the individual practices supporting the adherence of conduct to the code — that is to say, an ethical or ascetic morality whose normative aspect turns out to be quite rudimentary.

According to Foucault, the analysis of the ethical component of morality must consider four fundamental aspects, which Deleuze (1988, 102–03) traces back to the Aristotelian doctrine of the four causes: (1) the ontological aspect deals with the ethical substance — that is, that part of ourselves or of our behavior that is relevant for the ethical judgment in different historical moments (material cause); (2) the deontological aspect deals with the mode of subjection that specifies how individuals are urged to or incited to recognize their moral obligations and how the subjects are bound by their obligation to follow the code of conduct —that is, by divine law, natural law, rational rule — Kant-like universal norms — or by an aesthetics of existence (formal cause); (3) the ascetic aspect deals with the practice of self, that is, it indicates how to operate on the ethical substance (efficient cause); and finally (4) the teleological aspect deals with the *télos* of moral behavior (final cause).

The precept of self-care is the red thread guiding Foucault in his analysis of ancient ethics from the standpoint of an *an-archaeo-genealogical* problematization of the Christian ethical model. The discussion of the many facets and implications of the care of the self as the foundational rule of Greco-Roman individual and social behavior offers Foucault the opportunity to dwell on the four different aspects of ancient ethics. In Foucault's reading, the notion of the care of the self designates, at the same time, a general attitude towards oneself, toward things, and toward the world — we would say a specific way of *being-in-the-world* that requires turning one's own gaze inward to watch over what happens in one's own thought; and, at the same time, it involves "a number of actions exercised on the self by the self, actions by which one takes responsibility for oneself and by which one changes, purifies, transforms, and transfigures oneself" (Foucault 2005, 11).

In ancient morality, the aesthetics of existence is the characteristic mode through which the subject binds itself to a specific regulation of its *ēthos* (deontological aspect), and the care of the self is the framework, or better yet the horizon of sense providing its inspiring principle. The *aphrodisia* is the set of the acts related to pleasure, or the ethical substance (ontological aspect) whose regulation is targeted by the aesthetics of existence through a series of practices, exercises, and technologies the subjects put in place (ascetic aspect) to gain complete mastery over themselves (teleological aspect). Therefore, Foucault proposes an entire interpretation of ancient ethics that moves from the primacy of the notion of "care of the self." Traditional philosophical historiography had not acknowledged such primacy because its backward projection of the function that the hermeneutics of the subject performs in the Christian ethical model had led it to favor the Delphic precept of self-knowledge. It follows that a proper understanding of the meaning of "know thyself," of the Delphic *gnothi seauton*, and of self-knowledge in antiquity in general, becomes particularly important for Foucault's project of problematization of the Christian ethical model. Its analysis must start from the issue of the care of the self, since the latter provided the authentic ground from which it emerged:

> When the question of the relation between the subject and knowledge is posed in the culture of the self of the Hellenistic and Roman period, the question never arises of whether the subject is objectifiable [*objectivable*], whether the same mode of knowledge can be applied to the subject as is applied to things of the world and whether the subject is really part of these knowable things of the world. [. . .] there is the need to inflect knowledge [*savoir*] of the world in such a way that it takes on a certain form and a certain spiritual value for the subject, in the subject's experience, and for the subject's salvation. (Foucault 2005, 318)

In the Greek, Hellenistic, and Roman modes, asceticism [*askesis*] is certainly a practice of truth and a form of government of truth, but it does not imply the objectivation of the self within a true discourse. For the ancients, asceticism is neither a process of renunciation of the self nor a submission to the law. Rather, it is the process of gaining a preparation [*paraskeue*] for the future as well as a precise, full, and accomplished relationship of self to self. From this point of view, the problem is to what extent knowing and practicing the truth will allow subjects not only to act as they must, but also to be exactly as they must and want to be. The problem is to determine to what extent the exercise of truth may help the formation of autonomous subjectivities.

The hierarchical reversal between care of the self and self-knowledge represents for Foucault the distinctive character of the modern mode of subjectivation, which the Christian matrix and, to some extent, Western philosophy since Descartes has enabled. In fact, Foucault argues that, philosophically speaking, the modern age begins when knowledge becomes the only condition of access to truth and the bond between philosophy and spirituality is broken. From this standpoint, the deep connection for centuries binding philosophy and spirituality is based on the idea that subjects in and of themselves cannot have access to truth through simple acts of knowledge. Rather they must transfigure themselves to become capable of truth. Therefore, modern philosophy begins when that essential link ruptures and essentially transforms the relationship between subject and truth. Foucault identifies the "Cartesian moment" as the locus of that rupture. Obviously, he specifies, the rupture was not sudden, but one can find its origins in the internal conflict within Christianity itself: between spirituality and theology, asceticism and theology, and in the correspondence that Christian theology postulated between divine omniscience and the subjects' possible knowledge through faith. The philosophers of the nineteenth century ("Hegel, Schelling, Schopenhauer, Nietzsche, the Husserl of the *Krisis,* and also Heidegger") re-proposed, at least implicitly, the remote issue of spirituality and rediscovered the concern for the care of the self (Foucault 2005, 28).

Foucault also sees Marxism and psychoanalysis (especially Lacan's) as forms of knowledge concerned with spirituality understood as the transformation of a subject's being that will allow an access to truth. It begins when "the form of thought that asks what it is that enables the subject to have access to the truth and which attempts to determine the conditions and limits of the subject's access to the truth" and "the search, practice, and experience through which the subject carries out the necessary transformations on himself in order to have access to the truth" (Foucault 2005, 15). Foucault follows the evolution of the issue of *care of the self* from its entrance into the sphere of philosophical reflection — essentially tied to the figure of Socrates, "the master of the care of the self" — through the Greek and Latin philosophy of the first two decades after Christ (i.e., the phase of its undisputed climax), until its dissolution in Christian asceticism. In doing so, he reviews the moments, the texts, and the questions that were the building blocks of classical ethics determining both its development and its decline.

In its Socratic-Platonic treatment, the *care of the self*, while enjoying an undisputed primacy, in fact comes to coincide with self-knowledge. Self-knowledge represents both the first step and the fulfillment and sovereign form of the care of the self. Only through self-knowledge the subject comes to actually understand the self of which they must take care, making it possible to access truth in general. This follows, according to Foucault's reading, from the fact that the *care of the self* is considered fundamentally the necessary condition for the exercise of power. It is a principle reserved for young aristocrats destined to exercise political power because it is the prerequisite that would allow them to move from their condition of statutory privilege — their belonging to a socially privileged class — to specific political actions and the effective government of the city. The issue of the *care of the self* is, therefore, a pedagogical problem closely related to the theme of the ignorance that one ignores: ignorance about things that it would be necessary to know, and ignorance about oneself, since one does not even know one is ignorant of such things. Caring for oneself and caring for others are two reciprocally tied aspects of a single process: by acquiring the first skill, one also acquires the second one; for by saving myself, I save the city; and by saving the city, I save myself. Thus, an essential mutual implication links catharsis and politics, in Plato's thought. By taking care of itself putting into practice the catharsis of itself, the soul discovers its own being and uncovers its own knowledge as reminiscence, thanks to which it can contemplate the truths that will allow it to refound the city according to justice.

On the contrary, at the beginning of the imperial era, the care of the self frees itself from pedagogy and political activity reaching its golden age: it becomes a general unconditional principle, an imperative that is imposed on everyone, with no temporal constraints and regardless of social status.[6] The self is both the object and the goal of care itself, rather than functioning as a connecting and transitioning factor toward others and toward the city: "It was a matter of elaborating an ethics that enabled one to constitute oneself as an ethical subject with respect to these social, civic, and political activities, in the different forms they might take and at whatever distance one remained from them" (Foucault 1988b, 3:94). Since the *care of the self* no longer has a purely educational role and has become a lifelong commitment, the role of self-knowledge is greatly diminished, and the medical model replaces the pedagogical one. The critical function toward oneself, one's own cultural world, and others replaces the pedagogical function, and the model of permanent combat replaces the pedagogical model. In this context, asceticism assumes a central role, becomes independent from paideia, and is organized as a body of particular practices and exercises that are part of the virtuous life of the free man. Self-knowledge plays an important role in these exercises that aim at self-mastery, self-control, and sovereignty of individuals over themselves. The aim and purpose of the care of the self is the return to oneself — hence, the crucial importance of the notion of conversion.[7] It becomes one of the most important concepts in the technologies of the self known to the West, not only within Christianity, but also in moral philosophy. The development and organization of asceticism — what Hadot called *spiritual exercises* — and the tendency towards a universalization and codification of the ethics of care of the self (e.g., in the case of late Stoicism passes through the recognition of the self as a universal and rational being) show the path that will lead Christianity to the absorption and reworking of the Hellenistic ethical model. Just as the latter, says Foucault,

> was nevertheless the site for the formation of a morality which Christianity accepted, took into itself, and developed so as to make it what we now mistakenly call "Christian morality," and which at the same time it linked, precisely, to exegesis of the self. The strict morality of the Hellenistic model was taken up and shaped by techniques of the self that were defined by the specifically Christian model of self-exegesis and self-renunciation. This, if you like, is a bit of the general historical perspective in which I would like to place all this. (Foucault 2005, 258)

According to Foucault, the change that occurs with Christianity does not so much concern the content of the code, but rather it concerns the four aspects of the relationship with oneself that constitute the ethical component of Christian morality and are clearly connected with each other. The ethical substance is not made up of pleasure, but of desire, and the *télos* is no longer self-mastery so much as it is the purity and immortality of the soul, which is why asceticism takes the form of a hermeneutic of the self. Finally, the mode of subjection is that of divine law, which leads Christian ethics to conform to the juridical model and privilege the normative aspect of morality over a subject's relationship to self.

Foucault does not turn to ancient ethics out of a nostalgic desire to "re-actualize" a mythological past. Contrary to Hadot's claim, Foucault is not implicitly trying "to offer contemporary mankind a model of life."[8] Paraphrasing the Deleuzian quote that served as the epigraph to this chapter, we can say that the philosophical experiment Foucault conducts in these years deals with the historically determined possibilities of constituting ourselves as subjects, and not with a return to the Greeks.[9] As Catucci points out, the very idea of a "revaluation" of antiquity "is totally foreign to Foucault's archaeological and genealogical approach, which constantly invites us to distrust the similarities between the past and the present and rather to recognize the differences that make any attempt to 're-actualize' concepts or practices only nominally coinciding with the needs of the present essentially unfeasible" (2020, 150). In fact, far from uncritically assuming ancient ethics as an alternative solution to the problems of the contemporary world, Foucault stresses its limits and highlights its weaknesses. He emphasizes its elitist, virile, aristocratic — and also — its fundamentally self-contradictory character: "The Greek ethics was linked to a purely virile society with slaves, in which the women were underdogs [. . .] The Greek ethics of pleasure is linked to a virile society, to the dissymmetry, exclusion of the other, an obsession with penetration, a kind of threat of being dispossessed of your own energy, and so on. All of that is quite disgusting!" (Foucault 1982, 232–33).

On the other hand, Foucault sees the ethics of the *care of the self* as the attempt to think positively about the freedom of individuals and in a relation of immanence with respect to experience freedom: "is not defined as a right to be free, but as a capacity for free action" (Foucault 2011b, 310). In the ancient idea of an ethics conceived as stylistic research immanent to existence Foucault sees the possibility of an ethics for a practically conceived subjectivity. In the ancient form of individual and autonomous subjectivation understood as the search for a style of individual conduct in the relationship with oneself and with others, he glimpses the possibility of an ethics that is not normative, generalized, and unifying. An ethics that safeguards a space for an active and constructive exercise of individual freedom is an ethics that does not seek to constrain the subject within the metaphysical structure of identity: "Greek ethics is centered on a problem of personal choice, of aesthetics of existence. The idea of the *bios* as material for an aesthetic piece of art is something which fascinates me. The idea also that ethics can be a very strong structure of existence, without any relation with the juridical *per se*, with an authoritarian system, with a disciplinary structure. All that is very interesting" (Dreyfus and Rabinow 1982, 235). However, Foucault also recognizes that this very idea generates a contradiction when one tries to turn this individual style of existence into a style common to all. In the second and third centuries, such a style succumbs in the self-contradictory attempt to transform itself into a unified morality expressed in terms of code and truth.

Foucault considers ancient ethics a twofold tool of *problematization*. First, as we saw in this section, the problematization constitutes the concluding phase of the *an-archaeo-genealogical* process with respect to the modern mode of subjectivation, insofar as it brings to completion the relativization of a given reality and brings it back to its historical-conjunctural dimension. Second, as we shall see more fully in the next section, the problematization that ancient ethics makes possible serves to raise the problem of otherness and sets in motion the problematization of the function of philosophy. It clears the path for a questioning of the task and role of the philosopher and the intellectual, in which the thematization of *parrhēsia* plays an essential role.

Parrhēsia and Philosophical Alterity in Subjectivation Processes

The inquiry into the Greek concept of *parrhēsia* belongs to the research perspective that Foucault inaugurates with the notion of *government of truth*. The interest in such a concept depends, first of all, on the desire to test the positive and emancipatory potential of the notion that had proved to be an excellent hermeneutic-critical tool. In fact, the Greek model of *parrhēsia* offers Foucault the possibility of thinking of the government of men by the truth from the standpoint of the care of the self, rather than from pastoral power. The transversality of the concept of government of truth allows Foucault to highlight the intertwining of references and the reciprocal implications between the three dimensions of experience that constitute the space of processes of subjectivation. Whereas this intertwining is conceived exclusively in terms of subjugation in the analysis of the specific form of government of truth that characterizes the pastoral model, the *parrhēsiastic* model allows Foucault to think of it in terms of autonomous subjectivation. The *parrhēsiastic* model gives him the chance to interpret the *government of truth* in an alternative form. This is a form of the *government of truth* in which truth would neither be a dogmatic content, nor would it imply an obligation to a reflexive manifestation of truth. The model of *parrhēsia* represents a form of government that implies neither a relationship of obedience and subordination of the governed nor the technologies of the self aiming at binding the subject to a specific identity to better govern their conduct.

From this point of view, the first step consists of considering the possible role of otherness within the processes of subjectivation not as a subjugating force but rather as the instrument of an autonomous construction of subjectivity. Under what conditions can *others* be considered a mediating force in the process of autonomous subjectivation? I would say that Foucault's implicit answer is as long as they do not use truth either as an instrument of coercion or as a universal value to which the subject is nailed down and necessarily subjected — as long as the others turn truth into the principle of their own *ēthos* in conducting their action toward themselves and toward others. The crux of the ancient problematic of *parrhēsia* lies precisely in this condition, according to Foucault's reading. The exercise of *parrhēsia* is a form of *government of men by the truth* in which government is a relationship aimed at the constitution of individuals as autonomous subjects and masters of themselves. It is accomplished through the critical mediating function that the *other* operates within the process of subjectivation, in which truth is the means to problematize the real and grounding *ēthos* of the governing *other*.

At issue in Foucault's inquiry is, more or less explicitly, whether this particular interpretation of the *government of truth* may designate the task of philosophy. Foucault interrogates *parrhēsia* as philosophical *ēthos* to assess whether it is necessarily the philosopher who must assume the burden to play the role of *positive* otherness, under what conditions should this happens, and with what consequences. It is then a matter of determining whether such a function is exhausted by the critique of the regime of truth that determines the boundaries of the possibilities of subjectivation in a given conjuncture, and whether this function must and can be tested as a *political* exercise. Moreover, it is a matter of deciding whether this function exhausts the relationship between philosophy and politics.

Formally, Foucault's analysis of *parrhēsia* is articulated on three levels. He distinguishes between *parrhēsia* as alethurgical practice, philosophical *parrhēsia* as the specific *ēthos* of the philosopher in antiquity, and political *parrhēsia* as the practice of telling the truth in a political context. In fact, as I show in more detail in the following pages, these three levels tend to collapse onto each other, thanks to the transversality of the problematic related to the practice of *parrhēsia* that, although complex, turns out to be substantially unitary. The issue of *parrhēsia* concerns the *ēthos* that must characterize otherness in a relationship that is not oriented to the subjugation of the individual but rather to its autonomous subjectivation. Moreover, since the strategic function of otherness turns out to be fundamentally a critique of the regime of truth, the normative framework, and the techniques of subjection, we are clearly facing a problem that is always already political. The unity and substantial transversality of *parrhēsia* derive precisely from the close link that binds it to philosophy, as we will see more clearly later: "these are the three poles which are both irreducible and irreducibly linked to each other. *Alētheia, politeia, ēthos*: the essential irreducibility of these three poles, their necessary and mutual relationship, and the structure of the reciprocal appeal of one to the other, has underpinned, I believe, the very existence of all philosophical discourse from Greece to the present" (Foucault 2012b, 66).

At the same time, this very constraint means that when Foucault thematizes *parrhēsia*, he is actually questioning the exercise of philosophy. On January 12, 1983, during the second lecture of the course dedicated to *The Government of Self and Others*, Foucault defines *parrhēsia* as a "spidery notion."[10] *Parrhēsia*, Foucault explains, does not refer to a specific conceptual system or philosophical doctrine — it runs from one system to another, from one doctrine to another, and more importantly from one field to another. It moves from the individual direction of consciousness to the political field, and to religious experience. In

Foucault's eyes, what makes it a particularly fruitful terrain of inquiry is precisely such a position at the intersection of these different areas, which allows him to show how their mutual correlations are concretely realized. This is why, I believe, devoting so much space to the analysis of the different aspects and facets of the question of *parrhēsia* is also, for Foucault, an effort to test the philosophical outlook that he had been sketching out and probe its uncertainties, aporias, and contradictions:

> With the notion of *parrhēsia*, originally rooted in political practice and the problematization of democracy, then later diverging towards the sphere of personal ethics and the formation of the moral subject, with this notion with political roots and its divergence into morality, we have, to put things very schematically — and this is what interested me, why I stopped to look at this and am still focusing on it — the possibility of posing the question of the subject and truth from the point of view of the practice of what could be called the government of oneself and others. And thus we come back to the theme of government which I studied some years ago. It seems to me that by examining the notion of *parrhēsia* we can see how the analysis of modes of veridiction, the study of techniques of governmentality, and the identification of forms of practice of self interweave. Connecting together modes of veridiction, techniques of governmentality, and practices of the self is basically what I have always been trying to do. (Foucault 2012b, 8)

The first examination of *parrhēsia* occurs in the last part of the course devoted to *The Hermeneutics of the Subject*, within the context of the analysis of the care of the self in late antiquity and, in particular, regarding the Greco-Roman practice of the direction of consciousness.[11] Here, Foucault begins to explore the first level of the confrontation which keeps him engaged for the last two years of his life. At this more general level, he outlines the basic characters of *parrhēsia* as one of those alethurgical forms of manifestation of truth, with which he had dealt in the course *On the Government of the Living*.[12]

Parrhēsia consists of the pure, simple, and direct transmission of truth, but its truth content does not define it. Rather, the speaker's goal, when transmitting this content, is to create the conditions for the listeners to establish an independent, complete, and satisfactory relationship with themselves. The goal is to make the listeners internalize the true discourse that is addressed to them and make it redundant.[13] Therefore, *parrhēsia* does not really amount to "saying-it-all" as its etymology might suggest. It is not so much about getting out the whole truth as it is about the attitude of total freedom and openness in speaking it, for the speaker of *parrhēsia*, the *parrhēsiast*, can only choose to adopt that attitude in complete freedom. Above all, *parrhēsia* is defined by the fact that the teacher is always necessarily implicated in the truth that he decides to manifest and for which he has decided to assume full responsibility.

The only conditions for the exercise of *parrhēsia* are those that prudence and occasion, the *kairos*, dictate to allow truth to be received in the best way and at the best time.[14] Therefore, *parrhēsia* is, on the one hand, a free act of telling the truth that has no rhetorical constraints and must only take into account the specific situation and its listeners. On the other hand, it is a discourse that commits those who pronounce it to behave in perfect conformity to the truth they enunciated. According to Foucault, the foundation of Greco-Roman "psychagogy" lies in this very close link between enunciation of the truth and *exemplum*:

> If, then, we call "pedagogical" this relationship consisting in endowing any subject whomsoever with a series of abilities defined in advance, we can, I think, call "psychagogical" the transmission of a truth whose function is not to endow any subject whomsoever with abilities, etcetera, but whose function is to modify the mode of being of the subject to whom we address ourselves. [. . .] Let's say that within the psychagogical relationship, the essential burden of truth in Greco Roman Antiquity, that is, the necessity for telling the truth, the rules to which one must submit oneself in telling the truth, in order to tell the truth and so that the truth can produce its effect — namely, transformation of the subject's mode of being — falls essentially on the master, the guide, or the friend, or anyway on the person who gives advice. (Foucault 2005, 407–08)

The analysis of *parrhēsia*, Foucault argues, must emphasize not the utterance of truth but rather the act of the speakers who are placing themselves in what they affirm. The *parrhēsiastic* act commits the speaking subjects to a twofold pact with themselves. On the one hand, it implies they actually hold the truth they utter; and on the other hand, it implicitly binds them to what they say and to the very act of saying it. *Parrhēsia* is such because the irruption of true discourse creates an open situation and determines an indefinite risk for the subjects who speak and who, by speaking, assert their own freedom. There can only be *parrhēsia* if there is freedom in the enunciation of truth: the freedom of the act whereby the subjects speak the truth, and the freedom of the covenant whereby the speaking subjects bind themselves to their utterance and to their enunciation of the truth. There is *parrhēsia* when the act of speaking the truth entails burdensome consequences for the one who speaks it: *parrhēsia* entails a risk for the speaker. The *parrhēsiast* voluntarily and explicitly decides to tell the truth no matter the cost, even unto death: "*parrhēsia* is a way of binding oneself to oneself in the statement of the truth, of freely binding oneself to oneself in the form of a courageous act. *Parrhēsia* is the free courage by which one binds oneself in the act of telling the truth. Or again, *parrhēsia* is the ethics of truth-telling as an action which is risky and free" (Foucault 2011b, 66). The truth that the *parrhēsiast* brings into play is closely tied to current events — to *kairos*, or contingency in the strong sense. This is why the *parrhēsiast* questions specific actions and not general ethical principles, and this is why the *parrhēsiast* is always running a risk. *Parrhēsia* is a critical exercise toward oneself or toward others.

This brief discussion of the outline of Foucault's reading of *parrhēsia*[15] brings out the first problematic issues. Foucault's answer to the question about the role of otherness in autonomous processes of subjectivation suggests an alterity defined by a specific *ēthos* and a definite relationship of self with self. Neither the membership in a specific institution nor the possession of a title certifying the mastery of a specific type of knowledge, nor even an earned rank, or a political/social statute qualify a person for this otherness. It must only satisfy ethical conditions that are collected under the notion of *parrhēsia*. Therefore, the question is: who are the *parrhēsiasts*?

They are certainly philosophers, but only those philosophers that "subjectivize" themselves as such by establishing a relationship with themselves that begins with a reflected form of the practice of freedom — in other words, only those philosophers whose practice starts from ethical reflection. The identification between *parrhēsiasts* and philosophers is not ontological and universal, but rather it is contingent and individual. Since the *parrhēsiast* is committed to assume a specific *ēthos*, its identification with the philosopher is necessarily provisional and depends on how the *parrhēsiast* determines to act as a philosopher. First condition: the philosopher must achieve their processes of subjectivation in the form of an ethics. Subjectivation happens through the enactment of freedom as a form of critical thinking that problematizes freedom as it enacts it. Foucault suggests: " . . . what is ethics, if not the practice of freedom, the conscious [*réfléchie*] practice of freedom? [. . .] Freedom is the ontological condition of ethics. But ethics is the considered form that freedom takes when it is informed by reflection" (Foucault 1997a, 284). Second condition: the philosophers need to choose freely and deliberately the practice of *parrhēsia* as their own philosophical *ēthos* and as the form of their relationship with themselves as philosophers. This entails that the philosophers' duty is mainly *ēthopoiesis*: the task of the philosophical practice of telling the truth is the development of the individual *ēthos* and the individual's "free" subjectivation. The philosopher's discourse of truth must be oriented toward the transformation of an individual's subjectivation and must focus on an ethical constitution that would be autonomous from the subjugating forces to which it is already subjected.

On the one hand, not every philosophical exercise is *parrhēsia*; on the other hand, every exercise of *parrhēsia* must be philosophical. Unlike its merely moral or political counterparts, Foucault argues, philosophical discourse is such because its interrogations of *alētheia, politeia,* or *ēthos* always entail the other two poles and address the tensions binding them to each other. The essential transversality of *parrhēsia* undoubtedly satisfies this requirement. Meanwhile, *parrhēsia* is also necessarily philosophical because it implies an active exercise of freedom and autonomy, which only a philosophically constituted subjectivity can exercise.

The attitude of philosophical discourse is not necessarily *parrhēsiastic* because it may also have the form of prophecy, wisdom, or technical teaching. It all depends on how the three poles are connected and how the link unites them — that is, in terms of reconciliation, unification, or heterogeneity (Foucault 2012b, 66):

> There is, I think, a fourth standpoint in philosophy. It is the parrhēsiastic standpoint, which tries precisely, stubbornly, and always starting over again, to bring the question of truth back to the question of its political conditions and the ethical differentiation which gives access to it; which constantly and always brings the question of power back to the question of its relation to truth and knowledge on the one hand, and to ethical differentiation on the other; the standpoint, finally, which constantly brings the question of the moral subject back to the question of the true discourse in which this moral subject constitutes itself and to the question of the relations of power in which this subject is formed. This is the parrhēsiastic discourse and standpoint in philosophy: it is the discourse of the irreducibility of truth, power, and ēthos, and at the same time the discourse of their necessary relationship, of the impossibility of thinking truth [alētheia], power [politeia], and ēthos without their essential, fundamental relationship to each other. (Foucault 2012b, 68)

The otherness that must intervene to mediate the processes of subjectivation is therefore a philosophical otherness that exercises *parrhēsia*. As a result, a question immediately emerges: if the constitution of a free subjectivity autonomous from the relations of power and from the enforced regime of truth needs the critical mediation of such a philosophical and *parrhēsiastic* alterity, does this need not simultaneously introduce a principle of heteronomy and subordination? Can one consider such philosophical otherness as authentically and exclusively emancipatory, or does it conceal the risk of establishing an aristocratic principle based on the ethical-intellectual privilege of the philosopher?

A comparison between the *parrhēsiast* and *le maître ignorant* — the protagonist of a seminar given by Jacques Rancière a few years after Foucault's death — may help bring into focus the problematic nature of Foucault's philosophical alterity.[16] Foucault and Rancière share a critical view of the pedagogical model as a tool for preserving social power relations, just as they share a desire to find an alternative emancipatory model. This is why, somehow, they end up also sharing the intrinsic limitations of any model of emancipation that requires a mediation, which is therefore unable to free itself from a principle of heteronomy and from a desire to achieve liberation rather than practice freedom. Despite such similarity, it is immediately clear that Foucault's *parrhēsia* differs substantially from the universal teaching of Rancière's ignorant schoolmaster, whose emancipatory function is limited to drawing attention to the natural equality of all intelligences. The ignorant schoolmaster only suggests an alternative pedagogical model (in which the book represents an egalitarian bond between teacher and student) that replaces the naturally hierarchizing relation enforced by the model explanation. Foucault tries to free himself from the pedagogical model altogether, and he repeats on several occasions that the function of the *parrhēsiast* is not pedagogical but rather psychagogical: it does not seek to transmit a content; it has a critical and emancipatory function. However, Foucault's *parrhēsiasts* are bound to the truth content they speak and promote, and which exposes them to a risk. It is a responsibility that forces them, however, not to teach but to turn their *ēthos* into an instrument of exemplary manifestation of the very content they utter.

The tension between the psychagogical function and teaching within *parrhēsia* is apparent. Foucault himself highlights such a tension in the course of his extended discussion of the figure of Socrates,[17] who "is the *parrhēsiast*, but, once again, with a permanent, essential relationship to prophetic veridiction, the veridiction of wisdom, and the technical veridiction of teaching" (Foucault 2012b, 27). Socrates leads others to care for themselves through a specific philosophical *ēthos*, which also consists of "putting himself in the hands of the missing teacher (the *logos*)" (Foucault 2012b, 152) and considering himself (as well as others) ignorant and in need of taking care of that ignorance by listening to the logos. However, it is also clear that he is the guide and the one who asks the questions. This is why Rancière considers Socratism to be a perfected form of brutalization, which may seem close to universal teaching yet it keeps the student completely dependent on the questioning of the master.

In order to differentiate *parrhēsia* from the other subjugating modes of the *government of truth* — and especially from the pedagogical mode — Foucault insists on the element of risk inherent in the exercise of *parrhēsia*. He stresses that all *parrhēsiasts* are in a condition of inferiority with respect to their interlocutors since, by choosing to tell the truth and carry out a critique, they expose themselves to the interlocutors' reaction and to their decision to respect the pact or not. The *parrhēsiasts* open themselves, in other words, to the danger of jeopardizing the very relationship that made *parrhēsia* possible. Foucault plays up *parrhēsiastic* risk against the obedience characteristic of the pastoral model of *government of truth*, and he opposes philosophical *ēthos* as an instrument of manifestation of truth against the transmission of a content of knowledge as a mode of subjugation. In the end, the major difference between Foucault's and Rancière's proposals lies in the latter's attempt to elaborate a method of universal emancipation that adopts a political outlook to overturn the pedagogical mechanism; while Foucault's proposal moves precisely from the impossibility to frame emancipation within a political-normative horizon. This impossibility is the main issue lying at the core of Foucault's analysis of political *parrhēsia*.

In the 1982 to 1983 course *The Government of Self and Others* Foucault addresses the theme of *parrhēsia* and its development within the political context — in particular, the relationships between truth and politics and between truth and democracy — and the respective functions of philosophy and politics.

In fact, it is a matter of looking at the same problem from another angle and focusing on different aspects while showing, at the same time, that we are dealing with the same issue. In antiquity, the theme of *parrhēsia* lay at the core of the debate on the foundations, limits, and decline of Athenian democracy. While *parrhēsia* provides the foundation and the point of origin for democracy, it is also one of its characteristic features alongside *isonomìa* (i.e., the equality of citizens before the law), and *isegorìa* (i.e., the constitutional right of all citizens to speak in the assembly).[18] *Parrhēsia* is a condition for the proper functioning of political interactions, yet it is totally immanent to them. It concerns the actual exercise of power, and it makes the problems of the political game appear in their specificity, in particular those concerning the oversized influence that some citizens enjoy:

> *Parrhēsia*, the truth-telling of the political man, is what ensures the appropriate game of politics. The importance of *parrhēsia*, it seems to me, is found in this meeting point. At any rate, it seems to me that we find here the root of a problematic of a society's immanent power relations which, unlike the juridical-institutional system of that society, ensure that it is actually governed. The problems of governmentality in their specificity, in their complex relation to but also independence from *politeia*, appear and are formulated for the first time around this notion of *parrhēsia* and the exercise of power through true discourse. (Foucault 2011b, 159)

Democracy is the formal condition of *parrhēsia* because it grants equality to all citizens and consequently allows for their freedom of opinion and participation in decision-making. The superiority and influence exerted by those who take the floor and direct others through persuasion, however, provides its factual condition. The contradiction between these two aspects determines the intrinsically conflicting relationship between *parrhēsia* and democracy. There is no true discourse without democracy, but true discourse introduces differences into democracy that threaten its egalitarian structure: the superiority, or the influence exercised by those who take the floor to direct others through persuasion, represents the material condition of *parrhēsia*. Conversely, there is no democracy without true speech, for democracy can only function if those who exert their influence over others do so by means of a discourse of truth. Yet democracy threatens the very existence of true discourse. Indeed, the death of true discourse is inscribed within democracy: it must defend itself from individuals whose particular qualities tend to place themselves so much farther above other citizens to bring democracy into danger. This is why Greek philosophical and political thought, starting with Plato, offers a number of criticisms of democratic *parrhēsia* that focuses on whether democratic institutions should allow *telling the truth*. For Aristotle, *parrhēsia* has a difficult status in democratic institutions because democracy cannot contain any ethical differentiation among its speaking, deliberating, and deciding subjects. Generally speaking, a double displacement of *parrhēsia* is always necessary: political *parrhēsia* must always bind itself to individual *parrhēsia*, the only form that can introduce the *logos alethēs* [true discourse] into an individual's soul.

The other side of the crisis of *parrhēsia* — complementary to the criticism of democratic institutions — is the valorization of the relationship between the prince and his adviser as the privileged locus of truth-telling. Even though Greek thought does not lack representations of tyranny's intrinsic risk as a space of silence and flattery, there is an explicit acknowledgment that the relationship between the prince and his advisers is more favorable to *parrhēsiastic* practice than that between people and orators. This is because the soul of the prince — the soul of the leader as an individual — is susceptible to ethical differentiation. The soul of the prince can be persuaded and educated to an *ēthos* that makes him able to listen to the truth and to behave in accordance with it, consequently limiting his power. In other words, the rule of the prince depends on his constitution of himself as a moral subject. It is just the soul of the individual, understood as the place of his ethical development, that is both the immediate goal of *parrhēsiastic* practice, as well as the medium between truth and its effects on political practice and on the social body. This is why the very structure of democracy, insofar as it does not allow ethical differentiations, leaves no room for truth and its political operationalization.

Foucault's essential aim in his extended confrontation with the theme of political *parrhēsia* in ancient thought, whose main passages I have briefly reconstructed, is showing that the problem of political *parrhēsia* as a manifestation of truth in the political context — as *government of truth* — coincides with the problem of *parrhēsia* as the *ēthos* of an alterity that mediates the subjectivation process. The stakes are exactly the same, as well as the aporias. As we saw above, since any exercise of *parrhēsia* must be philosophical, what is always at stake is the need for a philosophical alterity that — thanks to the specific *ēthos* of *parrhēsia* — is capable of manifesting a truth that is essentially critical. Such a truth offers a possible path toward autonomous subjectivation; and so, it plays an emancipating function. It does not matter whether this subjectivation concerns a single individual or a group. What matters is that it is the truth, as a critical manifestation, that allows for their emancipation and always sets in motion their transformation: " . . . there is no establishment of the truth without an essential position of otherness; the truth is never the same; there can be truth only in the form of the other world and the other life" (Foucault 2012b, 340). Or again, we could say that there can be no active exercise of freedom that does not imply a re-subjectivation in the form of otherness; and that such subjectivation can only occur through the exercise of critique because there cannot be transformation without criticism. *Parrhēsia* is the *ēthos* of the philosophers who courageously exercise this critique aiming at an emancipative transformation of others, since they were able to emancipate themselves in the first place through a reflexive practice of freedom — that is, via an ethical reflection, which is first and foremost the exercise of self-critique that worked as mediation for their autonomous subjectivation.

This is how Foucault depicts the political responsibility of philosophy: a necessary relationship, which must never be mistaken for coincidence, between telling the truth and politics. This is also Foucault's answer to the Platonic interrogation about the philosopher's *ergon*, about the real substance of philosophy. Since its responsibility depends on the philosophers' ethical choices and on the mode of exercise of philosophy that the philosophers decide to put in place, it is clear that this relationship, though necessary, can neither be politically codified, nor can it become part of that normative horizon on which philosophical truth-telling must critically focus:

> It is essential for all philosophy to be able to tell the truth in relation to politics, it is important for all political practice to be in a permanent relationship with this truth-telling, but it being understood that the truth-telling of philosophy does not coincide with what a political rationality can and must be. Philosophical truth-telling is not political rationality, but it is essential for a political rationality to be in a certain relationship, which remains to be determined, with philosophical truth-telling, just as it is important for a philosophical truth-telling to test its reality in relation to a political practice. (Foucault 2011b, 288)

Thus, according to Foucault, even when Plato says that those who philosophize must exercise power, he does not mean that philosophical knowledge should constitute the law of political action and decisions, but rather that the practice of philosophy must represent the mode of being and subjectivation of the subjects who exercise power.

Critique as Philosophers' *Ergon*

The discussion of the relationships between philosophy and politics, and between philosophy and power, which emerged in the context of Foucault's long confrontation with the notion of *parrhēsia*, fall within the more general inquiry about the task of philosophy. It is the question that philosophy addresses to itself and always underlies every authentically philosophical thought. It is the question that every thinker must implicitly or explicitly confront. It is obvious that the general lines of a thinker's work and the different philosophical itineraries a thinker decides to undertake always already provide an implicit answer to this question.

Foucault's is no exception: indeed, we can say that the question about the task of philosophy is constitutive of the entire Foucauldian project. By itself, the project of a *practical philosophy* implies a radical questioning of philosophical work. The main focus of Foucault's research is the historicity of truth and subjectivation processes, as well as the *actuality* understood as the singular and contingent conditions, categories, and normative frameworks that determine how acting and thinking unfold at a given time. The path philosophy must follow then leads to a problematization of the historical a priori of possible experience, as well as to a critique of anthropological universals and its principles, formal structures, and natural and ahistorical conditions. This means philosophy must take on the task of enabling the exercise of freedom as resistance and transformation of the historical a priori, and as a discontinuity from the norm. Its task requires it to critically mediate the subjectivation processes allowing for the development of an autonomous subjectivation that is heterogeneous from the specific regime of truth in which it takes place. Clearly such a task is also political: or rather, perhaps, it implies a particular relationship between philosophy and politics. Indeed, the very relationship between philosophy and politics must be rethought from the standpoint of *practical philosophy*: the former must relinquish all efforts to provide a foundation, seek a limitation of power based on universal principles, or directly intervene on the contents of the normative framework.

The choice of *practical philosophy* as a horizon of thought entails the search for a new role for philosophical truth-telling over and against political practice, as Foucault clearly laid out in 1978 at a conference in Tokyo:

> Perhaps one could see that there is still a certain possibility for philosophy to play a role in relation to power, which would be a role neither of foundation nor of renewal of power. Perhaps philosophy can still play a role on the side of counter-power, on the condition that this role does not consist in exercising, in the face of power, the very law of philosophy, on the condition that philosophy stops thinking of itself as prophesy, on the condition that philosophy stops thinking of itself either as pedagogy, or as legislation, and that it gives itself the task to analyse, clarify, and make visible, and thus intensify the struggles that develop around power, the strategies of the antagonists within relations of power, the tactics employed, the foyers of resistance, *on the condition in sum that philosophy stops posing the question of power in terms of good and bad, but rather poses it in terms of existence.* (Foucault 1978d, 192 my emphasis)

The previous section showed how the work on *parrhēsia* allows Foucault to outline precisely the contours of a particular mode of philosophizing that is neither prophetic nor pedagogical, neither normative nor foundational, but can nonetheless address the real and current conditions determining the modes of existence of individuals. Essentially, the particular mode and function of philosophical practice that Foucault calls forth through the analysis of Greek *parrhēsia* is the critical mode, as we have seen already. This mode is thematized most directly on several occasions between 1978 and 1984, in particular through the threefold engagement with the Kantian text *Was ist Aufklärung?*[19] The first time

Foucault engages in an explicit discussion of Kant's text and the idea of critique is in a 1978 lecture: "Actually, the question about which I wanted to speak and about which I still want to speak: *What is critique*?" (Foucault 2003c, 261). At this time already — that is, four years before his reflections on critique became intertwined with the analysis of the Greek concept of *parrhēsia* — Foucault defines critique as an attitude, a virtue, or an *ēthos*. Critique is an attitude that looks at the relations between power, truth, and subject, and it opposes governmentalization, of which it is the necessary counterpart:

> If governmentalization is indeed this movement through which individuals are subjugated in the reality of a social practice through mechanisms of power that adhere to a truth, well, then! I would say that critique is the movement by which the subject gives himself the right to question truth on its effects of power and question power on its discourses of truth. Well, then!: critique will be the art of voluntary insubordination, that of reflected intractability. Critique would essentially insure the desubjugation of the subject in the context of what we could call, in a word, the politics of truth. (Foucault 2003c, 266)

The expression *politics of truth* clearly corresponds to what Foucault would call the *government of men by the truth* a few years later.[20] Modern governmentality builds upon the pastoral power model, the dominating and subjugating version of the *government of men by the truth*, whereas the exercise of philosophy in the critical mode builds on the *parrhēsia* model its emancipating and liberating version. In these years, Foucault has not yet defined critique as the characteristic attitude of philosophical otherness that plays an emancipatory function in the processes of subjectivation. So, he does not yet expressly define the task of philosophy and the mode of relationship between philosophy and politics. However, the texts of the two conferences cited here, held a month apart,[21] already show many of the distinguishing elements of Foucault's reflection on the task of philosophy as it is developed through the analysis of *parrhēsia* and the Kantian definition of Enlightenment. First, we encounter the problem of power, which must be posed "in terms of existence." To do so, philosophy must rethink how it relates to politics and must relinquish its prophetic or pedagogical attitude, as well as any legislative or censoring ambition; instead, philosophy must move toward an analysis of the game of power relations considered from the point of view of the actual strategies concretely at work. Second, we find the element of the courage that critique requires to emancipate itself as it moves from obedience to autonomy. And then, we find Solon, Plato, and the Cynics as examples of the three fundamental ways in which the role of the philosopher as anti-despot has been historically configured: the philosopher as legislator, as advisor, and as the philosopher who scorns power. In the 1980s, these figures — and others from ancient philosophy — will again play a role in Foucault's argument that the exercise of philosophy implies a specific *ēthos*, which is always both critical and transformative with respect to the historical political context in which it takes place. This relationship between philosophical *ēthos* and resistance, between critique and transformation, provides the new space in which Foucault attempts to locate the relationship between philosophy and politics, in perfect continuity with the overall framework of his *practical philosophy*. Precisely the overcoming of the distinction between theory and practice in a philosophy that is always already *practical* turns critique into an action that makes possible and, at the same time, already implies a transformation:

> And then, above all, I don't think that criticism can be set against transformation, "ideal" criticism against "real" transformation. A critique does not consist in saying that things aren't good the way they are. It consists in seeing on what type of assumptions, of familiar notions, of established, unexamined ways of thinking [. . .] so that what is taken for granted is no longer taken for granted. To do criticism is to make harder those acts which are now too easy. Understood in these terms, criticism (and radical criticism) is utterly indispensable for any transformation. (Foucault 2001c, 456–57)

Thought as such is no longer conceived as a set of universal representations directing empirical behavior and giving meaning to particular conducts. Thought is itself an action, or better yet, a reflective action that allows individual to question the implicit conditions of their own conduct and distance themself from their identity, which constitutes the internalized form of a heteronomous modality of subjectivation. Thought in its critical mode of operation enables the active exercise of freedom. Politics — broadly understood as the set of historically determined relations of power, strategic games of truth, and mechanisms of subjugation that constitute the heteronomous component of the subjectivation processes — gives philosophers a necessary double reference for the exercise of their critique. First, politics is the object that must be subjected to critique, the object of the mediating and emancipatory work of philosophy as it "tests its reality." Second, politics so understood is the conjuncture that the philosopher must always take into account; it is the *kairos*, the occasion that, as we saw, is the only condition limiting the exercise of *parrhēsia*. This is why Foucault says that the philosopher must tell the truth not about politics but in relation to politics: "The test of philosophy, on the contrary, the test of philosophy's reality, is not its political effectiveness; it is the fact that it enters the political field in its specific difference and has its own particular game in relation to politics" (Foucault 2011b, 229). This reference to politics must be understood from the standpoint of the essential link between Foucault's *practical philosophy* and actuality — a link that binds him, as he acknowledged, to Kant's *Aufklärung*.

Critique, as the counterpart to the exercise of government, does not correspond to an absolute ambition not to be governed, but it is always configured as the will not to be governed in a specific and historically determined form, or the will to be governed otherwise. Since the *an-archism* of Foucault's *practical philosophy* is directed against any principle positing itself as absolute, universal, and wanting to escape historicity, it can only reject the idea of a fundamental anarchism as the original ambition not to be governed.[22] For Foucault, "it is not a question of saying all power is bad, but of starting from the point that no power whatsoever is acceptable by right and absolutely and definitively inevitable" (Foucault 2016b, 78). One could say that Foucault's an-archism is always relative or that Foucault's *practical philosophy*, even though it proceeds from a "principle of anarchy," does not find its achievement in the political aspiration to an absolute anarchism. Critique must be an *an-archaeo-genealogy* of the regime of truth that determines the current form of the government of individuals in order to set the conditions for their emancipation.

At the beginning of the 1982 to 1983 course at the *Collège de France, The Government of Self and Others*, entirely devoted to *parrhēsia*, Foucault dedicates the entire lecture of January 5 to a new analysis of Kant's *Was ist Aufklärung?* Returning to a suggestion he had advanced in the 1978 lecture already,[23] Foucault says that "Kant seems to me to have founded the two great traditions which have divided modern philosophy" (Foucault 2011b, 20). The first one unfolded from the question about the transcendental conditions of true knowledge — that is, from the first *Critique* — and it became an analytic of truth; meanwhile the other one, which arose from the question about the *Aufklärung* and the text on the French Revolution, questions actuality and is configured as "an ontology of the present, of present reality, an ontology of modernity, an ontology of ourselves" (Foucault 2011b, 21). The first tradition corresponds to Anglo-Saxon analytic philosophy, while the second one — to which Foucault connects himself — is the tradition that includes philosophers ranging "from Hegel to the Frankfurt School, passing through Nietzsche, Max Weber etc., . . ." (Foucault 2011b, 21). With the question on Enlightenment (understood as a question on actuality) Kant, in Foucault's reading, inaugurates modernity as a possible relation to actuality that interrogates its differential characters and sees its concrete specificity as an element of historical discontinuity, rather than as a prelude or a fulfillment of its *télos*: "For the attitude of modernity — Foucault explains — the high value of the present is indissociable from a desperate eagerness to imagine it, to imagine it otherwise than it is, and to transform it not by destroying it but by grasping it in what it is" (Foucault 1984, 41). From this perspective, the question about actuality turns into a question about the historical conditions delimiting the field of our possible experience in a given moment. These are the conditions that philosophy must always consider in order to define its own particular task. Critique is the necessary *medium* we need not only to answer the question about actuality, but also to pose this question from the standpoint of discontinuity and transformation that Foucault defines as the modern attitude.

Foucault's analysis of the Kantian text on the Enlightenment meets his investigations of *parrhēsia* in stressing the necessity of a very close relationship with the present. This relationship is achieved through a critical *ēthos* pursuing emancipation and a transformation directed toward the conquest of autonomy in the active exercise of one's own freedom of thought and action,

> on the one hand, to emphasize the extent to which a type of philosophical interrogation — one that simultaneously problematizes man's relation to the present, man's historical mode of being, and the constitution of the self as an autonomous subject — is rooted in the Enlightenment. On the other hand, I have been seeking to stress that the thread that may connect us with the Enlightenment is not faithfulness to doctrinal elements, but rather the permanent reactivation of an attitude — that is, of a philosophical ethos that could be described as a permanent critique of our historical era. (Foucault 1984, 42)

In this 1984 English article, his last devoted to Kant's essay, Foucault sums up his recent view on the practical task of philosophy as *ēthos* and on the conditions and limits of its exercise. Philosophy must carry out "a critical ontology of ourselves" (Foucault 1984, 49) as historically determined individuals and must be oriented toward the identification of the limits of the constitution of ourselves as autonomous subjects to determine, at the same time, "the possibility of going beyond them" (Foucault 1984, 50) through a work on ourselves. According to Foucault's practical critique, limits are not universal and necessary but rather singular and contingent: they are what the practical historical work of the philosopher must constantly measure itself against. The reversal of Kant's transcendental critique is clear. For Foucault, it is not a matter of recognizing the limits of the normative horizon determining the possibilities of experience, but rather of trying, through philosophical work, to test the possibility of overcoming these limits and questioning them as historically determined and not necessary. From this standpoint, archaeology and genealogy are the critical tools this philosophical experience needs. Critique is *an-archaeological* because it seeks "to treat the instances of discourse that articulate what we think, say, and do as so many historical events. And this critique will be genealogical in the sense that it will not deduce from the form of what we are what it is impossible for us to do and to know; but it will separate out, from the contingency that has made us what we are, the possibility of no longer being, doing, or thinking what we are, do, or think" (Foucault 1984, 46).

Philosophy's essentially experimental character prevents it from putting forward any ambition of completeness and definitiveness — it must always come back to itself and submit itself to the test of actuality. However, Foucault does not think that philosophical work must also relinquish cohesion and generality. Research can be cohesive because it has always as its starting point human practices considered under their technological and strategic profile (i.e., the different forms of rationality that regulate and organize human actions and the various modes of human interaction with respect to the normative framework in which they take place). In turn, the articulation of research according to the three axes of experience (knowledge, power, and ethics) guarantees its systematicity. Finally, generality derives from the fact that historically singular experiences, as well as particular practice and discourses, are always connected to more general problems.

Foucault's *practical philosophy*, precisely because it is practical, cannot claim for itself anything other than the precariousness, contingency, and singularity it strives to highlight in every other experience and discourse. As it conceives itself as *ēthos*, *practical philosophy* must face each and every time the experience of its limits and must measure itself against the actual possibility of their overcoming. It must compare itself with specific practices, with determinate modes of subjectivation, and with concrete power relations. The historical conditioning and the necessarily practical vocation of philosophy entail that its critical task is never completed once and for all, and its function of mediation in the processes of autonomous subjectivation of individuals is never guaranteed. Philosophy must give up its foundational and totalizing ambitions and must act at the local, non-universal level. It must give up any normative or prescriptive claim. While heeding its critical task, *practical philosophy* must necessarily be *event based* and *an-archic*: since it presents itself as a questioning of the heteronomous order seeking the autonomous constitution of subjectivity, philosophical discourse cannot be a normative or a legislative exercise. However, critique is not simply just a *transgressive* practice: it is *an-archic* because it does not target a specific law but rather the normative order tout court, or yet better the normative order in its historically determined actuality. Philosophy must show that the internalized heteronormative instances that nail individuals to specific forms of subjectivation and to specific identities are neither universal nor necessary. They are merely the product of the present normative order internalized by individuals and "criticism — understood as analysis of the historical conditions which bear on the creation of links to truth, to rules, and to the self — does not mark out impassable boundaries or describe closed systems; it brings to light transformable singularities. These transformations could not take place except by means of a working of thought upon itself; that is the principle of the history of thought as critical activity" (Foucault 1984, 335–36). When it assigns to its thinking such a goal, the practical philosopher cannot help but accept the burden of an infinite critical task that is always twofold because it also implies the self-critical exercise of an an-archaeo-geneaology of its own thought.

Afterword

The Legacy of Foucault's *Practical Philosophy*

Paraphrasing Deleuze, *practical philosophy* names Foucault's thought considered "as a *whole*," the logic that drove him from one level to another, through a set of crises and conceptual shifts, "to discover power behind knowledge," and "to discover 'modes of subjectivation' beyond the confines of power" (Deleuze 1995, 84). Foucault's *practical philosophy* "is a matter of a line of displacement, that is to say not of a line of a theoretical structure, but of the displacement by which my theoretical positions continually change" (Foucault 2016b, 76). It is "a strange three-dimensional figure" (Deleuze 1995, 93) in which the interdependence and irreducibility of truth, power, and *ēthos*[1] organize the deep dynamic coherence of the historical becoming of thought. Foucault's *practical philosophy* does not amount to a coherent, stable, and self-contained philosophical system. It provides us neither with an ultimate theory of power, nor with a ready-made theoretical framework to apply to reality as to an inert object of inquiry. It does not deliver to us a handy set of extremely insightful predictions ready to be used to describe our present, provided that they undergo accurate scrutiny in search for potential mistakes, but neither can it be reduced to a convenient toolbox full of spare conceptual tools available to employ at will.

What kind of *legacy* then did Foucault's *practical philosophy* leave to us? What kind of *legacy* does a *line of displacement* leave? What kind of *legacy* does a logic driving through crises and shifts leave?

I believe the answer to these questions requires the same move through which Foucault approaches the question of power. For Foucault, the question of power is neither an ontological matter of a *what*, nor could it be the object of a pure phenomenology: it could only be addressed considering the *how* of its multiple concrete historical manifestations. Likewise, the question of *practical philosophy*, more than trying to identify certain specific ideas or concepts, needs to ask for the *how* of Foucault's way of doing and understanding philosophy. Indeed, although it does not let itself be codified in a normative methodology, a distinctive praxis of thinking emerges as one follows the dynamic and inherently plural Fouauldian experience of thinking to which the rich archive of published and unpublished materials testifies. In the same way Foucault has suggested that "philosophy stops posing the question of power in terms of good and bad, but rather poses it in terms of existence" (1978d, 192), he also invites us to stop posing the question of philosophy in terms of a theory of universal truths, *but rather to pose it in terms of existence*. In Foucault's *practical philosophy*, the political and the epistemological are reciprocally bound in an existential terrain that exceeds the separation of different domains and where historical discursive practices, and different acts of truths take place and produce effects of either coercion and subjugation or resistance and emancipation. Posing a question in terms of existence — it being the question of power or the question of philosophy — means opening the inquiry to both the necessary co-implication of multiple dimensions (epistemic, political, and ethical) and to the instability of historicity and contingence.

One could say that the legacy of *practical philosophy* amounts to foregrounding a concern with the historical relation of thought and existence, in its exposure to intersubjective relationships, and to the contingency of reality. And such a concern does not spare the self-critical perspective problematizing the role of philosopher and her relation to truth. In this sense, just like the question about modes of power is inseparable from an inquiry into historical regimes of truth and forms of subjectivation, the question about Foucault's *practical philosophy* is inseparable from an inquiry into the history and historicity of thought and into the form of philosophical subjectivation it produces. *Practical philosophy* demands that the so-called philosopher interrogates her own *ethos*, task, and work rather than as a transcendental exercise preliminary to the establishment of a truth-knowledge, as part of the experience necessary to mobilize the transformative force of truth-critique. As Daniele Lorenzini has shown[2] — for Foucault, the force of truth "does not arise from the truth itself in its structure and content" (Foucault 2016b, 97), nor does it depend only on the game establishing its epistemic parameters. It rather results from its relation to a normative regime that organizes its production within the historical domain of practical relations of *government of self and others*, that is a field of subjectivation processes. While in power relations the force of truth can work as a means of control and domination, the force of truth as critique mobilizes the resistance of self-government against the government of others. Overall, the legacy of Foucault's *practical philosophy* is precisely the transformation *of* thought, understood through the ambiguity of the passive/active genitive, both as an exercise of thinking that undergoes continuous trasnformations, and as the transformative power of thought. Foucault himself is both subject and object of such a transformation: "I'm an experimenter in the sense that I write in order to change myself and in order not to think the same thing as before" (Foucault 2001c, 240–41).

The transformative potential of *practical philosophy* depends on the critical force of truth of the *an-archaeo-genealogical* investigations through which Foucault inquires into the concrete historical multiplicity of the practices of government that combine and articulate the diverse techniques of different modes of power and, in so doing, transform one another. As Penelope Deutscher has aptly emphasized, although he "sometimes referred to modes of power as historically consecutive" (2017b, 18), "more generally, Foucault argued that the techniques of different modes of power could have multiple valences yet operate in tandem" (2017b, 23) and "also depicts technique playing concurrently multiple roles in different apparatuses, whose aims and strategies do not always accord" (2017a, 216). This historical combination of multiple techniques and modes of power into contingent strategies of government takes place on an existential ground of transformability. And it is on such a ground that one finds always already the condition of freedom.

In *Stop the Thief*, Catherine Malabou remarks how resistance, not power, is primary for Foucault, precisely as a function of the fact that for him "power, thought, praxis, trajectories, and personal experiences exist — and can only exist — by transforming themselves" (116) and "consequently, resistance itself is unpredictable, taking a contingent form, and always specific, engaged in the movement of its transformations" (116). The existential terrain of the processes of subjectivation, is where the critical activity of the philosopher *parrhēsiast* "brings to light transformable singularities" (Foucault 1984, 335–36) breaking the suture between subjection and subjectivation, between governmental subjectivation and self-government. The force of truth-critique of *parrhēsia* enables emancipation by signaling "the existence of another economy of power" (123) and the transformability of reality. The truth spoken by the *parrhēsiast* is the truth of the being-potentially-otherwise always already inscribed in contingency, that is, it is an "anticipation of alterity" already inscribed in the present. As Deutscher signals, a distinctive temporal character of critique "is manifested in Foucault's understanding of both archaeology and genealogy" (2017a, 210).

The alterity of the philosopher *parrhēsiast* is a vehicle of emancipation in so far as it testifies to the inherent potential of historical existence to be otherwise. To function as emancipatory alterity for others, that is, to show them the existential terrain of contingent transformability as condition for an active form of freedom understood as autonomous subjectivation, the philosopher is called to accomplish the critical transformative work first upon herself, since according to Foucault "these transformations could not take place except by means of a working of thought upon itself" (Foucault 1984, 335–36). In the very last section of the book, I suggested that *parrhēsia* presents two main risks, which Foucault seems to recognize yet not solve: the risk of relying on a *philosophical heroism* of the *parrhēsiast* as practical condition for the exercise of freedom and the risk of replacing the institutionalized heteronomy of the historical regime of truth with the charismatic heteronomy of the philosopher. One question is then how to further the legacy of Foucault's *practical philosophy* and its search for the critical conditions of an anarchic exercise of freedom avoiding both these risks. Is there the possibility of an emancipatory experience of alterity other than the one encountered in the truth spoken and testified by a speech act philosophical *parrhēsia* or by the Cynics' *bios*?

I believe that Malabou sends us in the right direction when she suggests that Foucault stops on the threshold of what she called the "non-governable" (142) understood as the limit of government as mark of its impossibility. Understanding the exercise of thinking from the standpoint of Foucault's *practical philosophy* and furthering its legacy means precisely embracing a philosophical praxis that engages with the non-governable. Engaging with the non-governable means engaging with that dimension of existence that exceeds all kinds of normativity and mastery, and cannot be captured by the processes of subjectivation, a dimension we can call *infrapolitical*.[3] Could one conceive of the encounter with such a dimension also precisely as an experience of the *other* and *otherwise* always already inscribed in the historical contingency of existence? Could such an encounter amount to an experience of freedom also enabling emancipation processes?

Answering these questions would call for another book, one that would bring Foucault's *practical philosophy* into a posthumous dialogue with other thinkers (i.e., Derrida, Heidegger, Nancy, Irigaray) and traditions (i.e., psychoanalysis, feminism, deconstruction) that have been close to him in many ways, as well as with more recent works in critical theory, black and gender studies that have already engaged and furthered his legacy in many productive ways (i.e., Butler, Hartman, Mbembe, Denise Ferreira da Silva). Through his admirable archival work, Stuart Elden has shown the importance that collaborative projects played in the development of Foucault's thought. And taking this collaborative aspect as essential to his *practical philosophy*, one can suggest that bringing his work in a productive posthumous dialogue with other thinkers — like, for example, Bennington, Deutscher, Erlenbush-Anderson, Islekel, and Malabou have done — is precisely the right way to engage with his legacy going beyond hermeneutical work and philological accounts.

Notes

Introduction

1. See https://lundi.am/The-Black-Masses-of-Michel-Foucault-the-Bullshit-of-Guy-Sorman.
2. Rovatti 2008, 116. *Dits et écrits* (volumes 2 and 4) were only published in 1994, on the occasion of the tenth anniversary of Foucault's death, but the publication of the volumes collecting all the *Collège de France* courses followed it rather quickly and was eventually completed in 2015. Seuil-Gallimard started with "Il faut défendre la société" in 1997 (Engl. tr. 2020), then *Les anormaux* in (1999) (Engl. tr. 2007); *L'herméneutique du sujet* in 2001 (Engl. tr. 2005); *Le pouvoir psychiatrique* in 2003 (Engl. tr. 2006); *Sécurité, territoire, population* in 2004 (Engl. tr. 2007); *La naissance de la biopolitique* in 2004 (Engl. tr. 2010); *Le gouvernement de soi et des autres* in 2008 (Engl. tr. 2011); *Le courage de la vérité* in 2009 (Engl. tr. 2012); *Leçons sur la volonté de savoir* in 2011 (Engl. tr. 2013); *Du gouvernement des vivants* in 2012 (Engl. tr. 2016); *La société punitive* in 2013 (Engl. tr. 2018); *Subjectivité et vérité* in 2014 (Engl. tr. 2017); *Théories et institutions pénales* in 2015 (Engl. tr. 2019).
3. And also, for instance, Butler 2002, 2005; Gros 2002; Pandolfi 2000; Fontana 2008.
4. Of course, "the whole" is not to be understood as a philosophical system or any sort of monolithic totality.
5. In this essay, Alessandro Fontana takes up what he had already stated with Mauro Bertani, in 1997, in the editors' note to the Italian edition of the 1975–76 course, "Il faut défendre la société," that started the publication of Foucault's lectures at the *Collège de France*: "Moreover, with respect to the 'architecture' of the books and to those 'lines of actualization,' as Deleuze defined them, represented by the interviews, the essential function of the courses seems to be this: to pose problems, to trace out paths, to sketch out analyses, in a sort of immediate proximity with the materials of the 'archives' and with the building site of the 'library.' In this way, the courses give us the problem in the process of its creation, they bring to light hypotheses whose validity must be verified, they show the method — if there is one — whose effectiveness must be checked. And it is precisely for this reason that Michel Foucault's courses so often reveal — without in any way compromising the pertinence of what is said, on the contrary — the character of 'urgency' of most of them, with their broken promises, their unexpected improvisations, their sometimes-excessive shortcuts and a few often unexpected developments." A little further on, the editors add: "In the courses, in the books,

in the interviews, the same themes, the same problems, the same interests break down and circulate, each however within a specific discursive regime, and according to particular modes of enunciation" (Foucault 1998, 235–36).
6. Note that the title of the original English edition is different: *Michel Foucault. Beyond Structuralism and Hermeneutics*.
7. See the interview with Duccio Trombadori: "Once my work is finished, through a kind of retrospective reflection on the experience I've just gone through, I can extrapolate the method the book ought to have followed — so that I write books I would call exploratory somewhat in alternation with books of method" (Foucault 2001, 241).
8. On this issue, see the editors' note to *Bisogna difendere la società* (Foucault 1998, 235–36) and Le Blanc and Terrel 2003.
9. See the remarks opening the book accompanying the exhibition "Foucault," held in the Belleville space in November and December 1985 (Ewald, Farge, and Perrot 1995).
10. On this subject, Deleuze states: "If Foucault's interviews form an integral part of his work, it is because they extend the historical problematization of each of his books into the construction of the present problem, be it madness, punishment or sexuality" (1988, 115).
11. On this subject, see the interesting essay by Robert Castel 1986; also Foucault 1980, 61–62; Foucault 1984, 67–69; Foucault 1996, 455–64; Foucault 1994b, nn. 359, 735–46; Deleuze 2014, 118–19; Brown 1998, 43; Bernini 2008, 5–6; Luce 2009, 177; Pandolfi 2000, 90–96.
12. "I think I have in fact been situated in most of the squares on the political checkerboard, one after another and sometimes simultaneously: as anarchist, leftist, ostentatious or disguised Marxist, nihilist, explicit or secret anti-Marxist, technocrat in the service of Gaullism, new liberal, etc. An American professor complained that a crypto-Marxist like me was invited to the U.S.A., and I was denounced by the press in Eastern European countries for being an accomplice of the dissidents. None of these descriptions is important by itself; taken together, on the other hand, they mean something. And I must admit that I rather like what they mean. It's true that I prefer not to identify myself and that I'm amused by the diversity of the ways I've been judged and classified. Something tells me that by now a more or less approximate place should have been found for me, after so many efforts in such various directions; [. . .] I have to be convinced that their inability to situate me has something to do with me. And no doubt fundamentally it concerns my way of approaching political questions. It is true that my attitude isn't a result of the form of critique that claims to be a methodical examination in order to reject all possible solutions except for the one valid one" (Foucault 1984, 383–84).
13. It is no coincidence that Remo Bodei (1986) used the German term as an explicit reference to the Heideggerian tradition.
14. "*Foucault's refusal to elaborate a theory of power* follows from his insight that theory only exists and is only intelligible when it is set against and

among particular cultural practices. This is perhaps why he so often restricts his general comments on power. Instead, he has presented a systematic analysis of technologies of power for which he claims a certain significance and generality, although as a characterization these comments appear still appear to be rather all-encompassing and mysterious" (1982, 188, my emphasis).
15. "The work of Michel Foucault is still very much 'in progress.' Although the major contours are clear, his future writing is sure to contain unexpected twists and turns" (1982, 205).
16. For example, Dominique Janicaud pointed out that "Habermas imputes to Foucault the desire to construct a theory of power which would arrive at definitive and complete 'solutions'; it is as if he is attributing to Foucault the project of completing a systematic philosophy, as if Dreyfus and Rabinow (the merits of whose work I by no means wish to call into question) were more familiar to him than Foucault's actual questions" (1992, 295).
17. Herbert Nilson is implicitly referring to this interpretation when he points out, at the beginning of the third chapter of his work, that "[o]ne of the main reasons why Foucault's last studies on an ethics and aesthetics of existence were viewed with so much suspicion and surprise lies in the often-asserted thesis that Foucault's primary interest was in the development of an analysis of power phenomena. Foucault himself denied this thesis" (1998, 63).
18. However, I think I should give credit to Paul Rabinow, who acknowledged — in the preface to the 2010 edition — the great importance of Foucauldian research in recent years. His remarks strengthen the hypothesis of the excess of proximity as the main factor behind the original interpretation, although the tone of the preface remains essentially biographical and does not substantially challenge the theses the authors defended thirty years earlier.
19. For a detailed and articulated survey of the critical reception of Foucault's work before and after 1994, see Bernini 2008, 15–33.
20. See chapter 1 and note 22.
21. Although "objectification" is a common translation of the French objectivation, I consistently use "objectivation" to keep in focus the symmetry with "subjectivation" that is important to Foucault, as well as the equally important albeit implicit reference to "subjection" contained in the latter term, which would have been lost with the "subjectification"/ "objectification" pair.

Chapter 1

1. See Caruso 1999, 89ff. On this topic, see also Álvarez Yáguez 1995, pp.155–57.
2. See Caruso 1999; Foucault 1984, pp. 333–39; Foucault 1996, pp. 465–73; Foucault 2016, p. 202.
3. Deleuze (2014, 156–57); Thomas Flynn has suggested that Foucault's last genealogical investigations can still be considered as carrying out

Nietzsche's project of historicization of the subject (Flynn 1985, 535). On the relationship Nietzsche/Foucault in general see Sluga (2005, 2010). On Foucault's conception of subjectivity see Mark Kelly (2013).

4. Foucault left the French Communist Party (PCF) in 1953 and broke definitely with Marxism before leaving for Sweden in 1955. He remained close to Althusser, though. See Eribon 1991, pp. 50–60, esp. pp. 57–58. Eribon reports that Foucault, in a 1968 interview, contrasted the "dynamic and rejuvenated Marxism practiced by Althusser's students" to the "flabby, dull, humanist Marxism that Garaudy defended" (1991, 166).

5. For more details on Foucault's relationship to Marx, see Bernini 2008, pp. 38–55; Sheridan 1980, pp. 197–217; Luce 2009, pp. 98–104; Álvarez Yágüez 1995, pp. 33–35.

6. For instance, see Foucault 2007, p. 158.

7. See Foucault 2020, 5ff.; Foucault 2001, p. 111.

8. See Foucault 1970, pp. 272–87. In the section devoted to David Ricardo in *The Order of Things*, Foucault presents Marx's thought as a second yet derivative attempt to address the issue that animated the new episteme spreading throughout the West from the end of the eighteenth century onward — the relationship between anthropological finitude and history — within the confines of economics.

9. See Foucault 2001, p. 111; Foucault 2016, p. 22; Foucault 2012; 2016, pp. 11–12. See also chapter 3.

10. See chapter 2.

11. Bernini remarks that Foucault is probably referring to "those variants of Marxism such as, on the one hand, Freudian Marxism (Marcuse and Reich), and, on the other hand, the Althusserian theory of state ideological apparatuses" (2008, 110).

12. See chapter 2.

13. See the last section of this chapter.

14. In a 1982 interview, Foucault stated: "What I have studied are the three traditional problems: (1) What are the relations we have to truth through scientific knowledge, to those 'truth games' which are so important in civilization and in which we are both subject and object? (2) What are the relationships we have to others through those strange strategies and power relationships? And (3) what are the relationships between truth, power, and self? I would like to finish all this with a question: What could be more classic than these questions and more systematic than the evolution through questions one, two, and three and back to the first? I am just at this point" (Foucault 1988, 15).

15. In a 1975 conversation with Los Angeles students, Foucault stated: "I use the word archaeology for two or three main reasons. The first is that we can play with the word archaeology. *Arché* in Greek means beginning. We also have the word 'la arché' [sic] in French. The French word signifies the way in which discursive events have been registered and can be extracted from the archive" (Foucault 1978, 10).

16. For a more extended discussion of the link between the present and Foucault's analyses, see the discussion of the issue of critique in chapter 4.
17. Lorenzini, pp. 37–39.
18. See chapter 4.
19. See chapter 4.
20. See chapter 4.
21. See introduction.
22. I am referring to the contemporary re-proposition of the Aristotelian concept that took place in Germany in the 1960s and 1970s and was named so after the title of a well-known collection edited by Manfred Riedel. Among the participants to the debate were Hannah Arendt, Hans-Georg Gadamer, Hans Jonas, and Joachim Ritter. It is not by chance, according to Franco Volpi, that they were all following the 1918–1928 Heidegger's Freiburg and Marburg's seminars where Heidegger developed his "hermeneutics of facticity" on the basis of a reinterpretation of Aristotle's ethics. On this theme see Berti (1990, 1992); Volpi (1986); da Re (1986, 2001); Pacchiani (1980).
23. See Foucault 1988, p. 14: "What I react against is the fact that there is a breach between social history and the history of ideas. Social historians arc supposed to describe how people act without thinking, and historians of ideas are supposed to describe how people think without acting. Everybody both acts and thinks. The way people act or react is linked to a way of thinking, and of course thinking is related to tradition."
24. See chapter 3.
25. See also Butler 2002.
26. See chapter 4.
27. See chapter 4.
28. See, for instance, Remo Bodei: "The decision is taken to renounce the ideological dimension of the 1960s and 1970s. Foucault moves farther and farther away from politics (and from the traditional positions of the Left) and comes closer to erudition and to the 'genealogy of intempestivity,' as if he wished to underline the distance the intellectual must keep from the immediate present" (Bodei 1986, 916).
29. See, for instance, McGushin 2007; Nilson 1998; Rayner 2010; Montinari 2009.
30. See, for example, Edward F. McGushin, Thomas Flynn, Richard Lync, and Marta Faustino.
31. See chapter 4.
32. See chapter 4.

Chapter 2

1. See Deleuze 2014, pp. 131–32; and Deleuze 1995, pp. 97–98.
2. I retrace Foucault's speculative itinerary starting from the introduction of the knowledge-power pair, until its abandonment in favor of the notion of

"government by the truth," — an issue that will be addressed in the next chapter — and I will highlight the role the analysis of biopower and governmentality played in that development.

3. "Thus disciplinary mechanisms date from ancient times but in an isolated, fragmented manner, until the seventeenth and eighteenth centuries, when disciplinary power is perfected in a new technique with the management of men" (Foucault 2007, 146).

4. Foucault offers just a few remarks about Wilhelm Reich and Herbert Marcuse in addition to Freud.

5. In the first few lines of the course, Foucault reflects on his first five years at the *Collège de France* and on the research he has completed, which he is trying to come to terms with: "It seems to me that we could justify the work I have been doing, in a somewhat empirical and haphazard way both on my part and yours, by saying that it was quite in keeping with a certain period; with the very limited period we have been living through for the last ten or fifteen years, twenty at the most. [. . .] this has been a period characterized by what we might call the efficacy of dispersed and discontinuous offensives" (Foucault 2003, 5). He goes on to cite the effectiveness of the battles against the psychiatric institution as an example.

6. Such a thesis is a kind of historical paradox, because it emerges precisely at the threshold of modernity, when the medieval development of the European states has turned war into a state affair, moved it beyond a community's borders, and removed it from the body politics.

7. At first glance, Hobbes seems to be the philosopher who held war relationships as the foundation and principle of power relations. However, for Hobbes primitive war is born and develops in equality: it is the immediate effect of non-difference that prevents the establishment of relations of force. The Hobbesian state of nature is in fact not brutal at all: rather, the confrontations are calculated and emphatic representations of the forces at play, in a temporally indefinite relationship of fear. It is not war, but a "state of war." The principle that politics is war continued by other means is much earlier than Clausewitz's formulation, who simply reversed a widespread and at the same time precise thesis that had been circulating since the seventeenth and eighteenth centuries.

8. Foucault used the concept of biopolitics for the first time during the second of two lectures he gave at the Institute of Social Medicine of the State University of in October 1974 ("The Birth of Social Medicine"). The lectures were first published in the *Revista centroamericana de Ciencias de la Salud* and are now available in English in (Foucault 2004) and (Foucault 2003, 319–37), respectively.

9. Since some critics attacking Foucault for his too broad, erroneous, or at least questionable historical periodization fail to consider this, I think it is important to note that such a periodization come mostly from Foucault's lectures at the *Collège de France*, rather than from a study completely revised and formalized in a book (see the Introduction).

10. In *Foucault's Futures*, Penelope Deutscher aptly points out a problematic split in the secondary literature between studies concerned with Foucault's analyses of sexuality and studies interested in his account of biopolitics (2017, 2; 68–69). Such a division impeded a thorough discussion among Fouldaldian scholars, with the exception of Jasbir Puar *Terrorism Assemblages*, of reproduction as intersection between sexuality, racial hierarchies and the biopolitics of population. Overall, Deutscher engages compellingly with Foucault's procreative hypothesis drawing attention to its relation to the thanatological implications of biopolitics, and furthering and integrating Foucault's analyses – along with those of Giorgio Agamben, Roberto Esposito, Lee Edelman, and Judith Butler – to understand the attacks on women's reproductive power in terms of governmentalities of life associated with futurism.
11. The apparatus of sexuality also plays an essential function within another power-knowledge mechanism that is crucial to the exercise of biopolitics: state racism. It refers to the technologies of normalization that seek to regulate the general reproductive phenomena and sexual mores of a population. Racism constitutes the mediating term between a politics that is applied first and foremost to the creation of life and the exercise of the power of death. It grants power the possibility to exercise the old sovereign right to kill even within the horizon of normalization. In Foucault's analysis, the sexuality apparatus offers the possibility to introduce elements of discontinuity and separation within the biological unity of the population. Ultimately, it makes it possible to determine whose group's life it is necessary to sacrifice to ensure the life of another. As Foucault himself asks at the conclusion of the 1974 to 1975 course: "How can one make a biopower function and exercise the rights of war, the rights of murder and the function of death, without becoming racist? That was the problem, and that, I think, is still the problem" (Foucault 2020, 263).
12. Foucault 2007, 85 and 91. On this topic, see also Bernini (2008, 169), Zanini (2006, 123), and Luce (2009, 139).
13. See Pandolfi (2006) for detailed discussion of the issue of population.
14. All the different levels of the problem of government are brought to the forefront by the intersection of two major historical processes: the transition from feudal structures to large territorial states (i.e., the movement toward state concentration), and the Reformation vs. Counter-Reformation dialectic, which was a movement of religious dispersion and dissidence.
15. Foucault refers to Giovanni Antonio Palazzo's definition in (Palazzo 1604).
16. Foucault traces the birth of the *raison d'État* to the critical debate against Machiavelli's *The Prince*, whose goal is to oppose the transcendent singularity of the prince to the immanent and multiple action of government, and to promote the state conceived as a set of men and things and not as a territory. See Foucault 2007, pp. 320–23.
17. Neither the problem of the origin of the state (vs. Machiavelli), nor that of an external end such as salvation are posed (vs. Aquinas): "We now find ourselves in a perspective in which historical time is indefinite, in a perspective

of indefinite governmentality with no foreseeable term or final aim. We are in open historicity due to the indefinite character of the political art" (Foucault 2007, 341–42).
18. Europe, Foucault points out, is understood here according to an absolutely new idea: as a well-demarcated geographical construction that lacks universality and is fundamentally plural.
19. On this topic, see Foucault 2007, pp. 69–71 and Foucault 2010, pp. 65–68.
20. Foucault suggests that the principle of the totalitarian state, far from being an endogenous intensification and an extension of state mechanisms, is to be found in the party governmentality that makes its appearance in Europe, entirely unprecedented, at the end of the nineteenth century (Foucault 2010, 191).
21. In fact, there is no theory of the *homo oeconomicus* until the so-called neoclassic economists Walras and Pareto. However, the theory of the subject that the English empiricism advanced contains some uses of the term already. For the first time, a subject is not defined starting from its freedom, or from the opposition between soul and body, but rather as a subject of individual, irreducible, not transmissible, atomic choices unconditionally referred to the subject itself and to what is called *interest*.
22. "The situation of *homo œconomicus* could therefore be described as doubly involuntary, with regard to the accidents that happen to him and with regard to the benefit he unintentionally produces for others. It is also doubly indefinite since, on the one hand, the accidents upon which his interest depends belong to a domain that cannot be covered or totalized and, on the other, the benefit he produces for others by producing his own benefit is also indefinite and cannot be totalized" (Foucault 2010, 278–79).
23. Foucault points out that starting with this conception, the political problem of the use of genetics as a means of improving and increasing human capital opens up (Foucault 2010, 228).
24. "So, we have been trying out this notion of governmentality and, second, seeing how this grid of governmentality, which we may assume is valid for the analysis of ways of conducting the conduct of mad people, patients, delinquents, and children, may equally be valid when we are dealing with phenomena of a completely different scale, such as an economic policy, for example, or the management of a whole social body, and so on" (Foucault 2010, 186).

Chapter 3

1. For a general survey of Foucault's analysis of pastoral power see Pandolfi (2000, 230–32). Pandolfi analyzes the implicit Nietzschean inspiration of the theme of the pastorate in Foucault, in particular with regard to the adoption of a genealogical point of view on the beginnings of pastoral power.

2. Scientific discourse's assumption of truths coming from the device of confession did not occur without epistemological discussions and paradoxes and it required positing a number of principles and methodical adjustments. Foucault isolates five procedures through which confession is transposed into scientific forms, it is grafted onto the methods of clinical listening, and it develops into a *scientia sexualis*. The first step is a clinical codification of "making people talk" (i.e., the union of the mechanism of confession with that of clinical examination and the required identification of scientifically observable signs and symptoms). It is then a matter of introducing the postulate of a general and widespread causal power related to sex. In order to justify the techniques of confession, it is necessary to establish the principle of a latency intrinsic to sexuality: the truth of sex must be considered obscure and elusive by nature in order to ground into a scientific practice the need to wrest it from a subject who would like to hide it. Then, it is necessary to associate the confession with a method of interpretation that the collector of the confession must deploy in order to complete the truth he receives and fully bring it to light. The last step is the medicalization of the effects of confession — that is, it is a recodification and a transposition from the religious register of sin and penance to the medical register of the dichotomy between normal and pathological.
3. See Tokyo Lectures of April 1978 (Foucault 1999), (Foucault 1982), and the 1979 "*Omnes et singulatim*" Tanner Lecture at Stanford University (Foucault 2003, pp. 180–201).
4. In Foucault 2007, pp. 186–98 and in the lecture "Omnes et singulatim" (Foucault 2003, pp. 180–201), Foucault reports on the few exceptions in Greek and Latin texts where the metaphor of the flock-shepherd relationship recurs in the political sphere. First, such a metaphor is found in Homeric texts, in both the *Iliad* and the *Odyssey*. Secondly, a whole series of texts from the Pythagorean and neo-Pythagorean traditions refer to the theme of shepherding (Foucault refers to the fragments of the pseudo-Archita cited by Stobeo). Finally, Foucault considers references to the shepherd as a model of the magistrate in Plato's texts (*Critias, Republic, Laws*, and in the *Statesman*). Only in the *Statesman* does Plato discuss the topic at length, concluding that we must not turn to the metaphor of the shepherd to grasp what a politician really is. From the review of these texts, the conclusion Foucault advances, and leaves open, is that the theme of shepherding remains a purely Eastern theme, yet sufficiently well-known to be considered worthy of discussion.
5. In the Hebrew pastorate, only God is the true shepherd of his people, with the sole exception of King David who, as founder of the monarchy, received his task directly from God and participated in a subordinate shepherding role.
6. See chapter 2.
7. Foucault resorts to the creation of the word alethurgy from the Greek adjective *alethourgicus*. It was used by Heraclides, a grammarian of the second

or third century, to designate someone who tells the truth. Foucault's particular way of drawing the boundaries of the semantic field of this term recalls the use of a philosophical etymology of Greek terms that is a constitutive moment of Heideggerian research. With the word *alethurgy* Foucault is interested in bringing into play the double reference, on the one hand, to truth understood as the result of an unveiling act (as per the well-known Heideggerian etymology of the term *aletheia*), and, on the other hand, to the term liturgy [*leitoutgía*] with which it clearly resonates.

8. On the Foucauldian analysis of Sophocles's tragedy, see Brindisi (2010, 159ff.) and Cremonesi (2005).

9. Foucault devotes the end of lecture 5 and lecture 6 to the issue of the preparation for baptism, and in general to the relationship between purification and access to truth in Tertullian. In lecture 7 he addresses the question of the catechumenate as an authoritarian reorganization of the practices of catechesis and preparation for baptism. Starting with the eighth lecture (February 27), Foucault devotes himself to the analysis of canonical and ecclesiastical penitence practices between the end of the second and fifth centuries, highlighting the internal tension within Christianity between the perspective of conversion and salvation and the repetition of sin. The ninth lecture and part of the tenth deal with the issue of penance and the practice of exomologesis. Finally, lectures 11 and 12 are devoted to the direction of conscience in the context of monasticism and to the practice of *exagoreusis*.

10. The penitent, though excluded from many rites or ceremonies, does not cease to be a Christian and may be reintegrated into the community.

11. Foucault emphasizes that this is not remission of sins. See lesson 9.

12. In fact, it does not seem a coincidence that Foucault used an anecdote of undoubted impact when he introduced the same theme in the conferences that he held in the United States the following fall. It concerns the treatment the French psychiatrist François Leuret reserved to one of his patients: "One morning, Dr. Leuret takes Mr. A., his patient, into a shower room. He makes him recount in detail his delirium. 'Well, all that,' says the doctor, 'is nothing but madness. Promise me not to believe in it anymore.' The patient hesitates, then promises. 'That's not enough,' replies the doctor. 'You already made similar promises, and you haven't kept them.' And the doctor turns on a cold shower above the patient's head. 'Yes, yes! I am mad!' the patient cries. The shower is turned off, and the interrogation is resumed. 'Yes, I recognize that I am mad,' the patient repeats, adding, 'I recognize because you are forcing me to do so.' Another shower. Another confession. The interrogation is taken up again. 'I assure you, however,' says the patient, 'that I have heard voices and seen enemies around me.' Another shower. 'Well,' says Mr. A., the patient, 'I admit it. I am mad; all that was madness'" (Foucault 2016, 19). This is, in one way, an example of what Foucault cites as "truth therapies." He tells us that multiple examples may be found in the medical literature of the seventeenth and eighteenth centuries, which held that madness could be cured by demonstrating to the patient the incompatibility between

his delirium and reality. The episode Foucault recalls, however, goes far beyond the persuasive intent: in this case the psychiatrist aims at the verbal recognition of madness and at the explicit confession of the truth about himself by the patient. Foucault uses this account to bring out the postulate that one needs for his own salvation to know as exactly as possible who he is and also, which is something rather different, that he needs to tell it as explicitly as possible to some other people (Foucault 2016, 20).

13. Martyrdom is the most important model the Church Fathers used to justify the need for this practice: "The martyr is he who prefers to face death rather than to abandon his faith. The sinner abandons the faith in order to keep the life of here below; he will be reinstated only if in his turn he exposes himself voluntarily to a sort of martyrdom to which all will be witnesses, and which is penance, or penance as *exomologēsis*" (Foucault 2016, 60).
14. On this theme, see Bodei (1986, pp. 909–11).

Chapter 4

1. Deleuze's translators use *subjectification* for the French term *subjectivation*, while Foucault's generally use *subjectivation*. I changed all Deleuze's translations to use the latter term for consistency.
2. See Foucault 1970, 2013 (2X), 2012.
3. See Foucault 1978 (2X).
4. Foucault 1990, 1988.
5. Foucault 2011, p. 5. See, also, Foucault's statement in the 1983 interview with Dreyfus and Rabinow: "Three domains of genealogy are possible. First, an historical ontology of ourselves in our relations to truth through which we constitute ourselves as subjects of knowledge; second, an historical ontology of ourselves in relation to a field of power through which we constitute ourselves as subjects acting on others; third, an historical ontology in relation to ethics through which we constitute ourselves as moral agents. So, three axes are possible for genealogy. All three were present, albeit in a somewhat confused fashion, in the Madness and Civilization. The truth axis was studied in *The Birth of the Clinic* and in *The Order of Things*. The power axis was studied in *Discipline and Punish* and the ethical axis in *The History of Sexuality*" (Dreyfus and Rabinow 1982, 237).
6. The care of the self is generalized as an unconditional principle and as a rule that everyone can practice, although it remains a sectarian phenomenon that is always enacted within exclusive forms. It is linked either to religious groups and to specific cults — its popular aggregation point — or to the complex social network of friendship characteristics of Roman society — its cultured and sophisticated counterpart. Moreover, its new form radically changes the relationship between the few and the many, which loses its hierarchical character based on birth and acquires an operational one concerned with the relationship that the individuals entertain with themselves.

7. When dealing with the theme of conversion, Foucault makes direct reference to the research of Pierre Hadot and in particular to a text in which Hadot points to the opposition between the Platonic model of *epistrophé* and the Christian model of metanoia as the scheme needed to effectively understand the notion of conversion and its importance in Western culture. Plato's conversion (*epistrophé*), which consists fundamentally in turning away from appearances and returning to oneself through the care of the self in order to reach recollection and truth, is dominated by the rigid opposition between this world and the world of ideas. It is governed by the theme of the liberation of the soul from the body, and it is guided by the privilege of knowledge. Christian conversion (metanoia), on the other hand, occurs as a sudden change. It is a unique event that comports a transition and produces a caesura, a rupture in the subject. In Hellenistic and Roman culture, the conversion follows a very different model from both the "know thyself" of the Platonic *epistrophé* and the "examine yourself" of Christian metanoia. In Epicurean, Cynic, and Stoic thought, conversion occurs in the very immanence of the world itself: it does not allow a liberation from the body, but a more complete relationship with oneself. It is a process that concerns more exercises and practices than knowledge. Turning one's gaze towards oneself means, on the one hand, turning it away from others, from daily life and from curiosity, and, on the other hand, turning it away from the world.
8. When pointing out the differences between his and Foucault's analyses of spiritual exercises, Pierre Hadot — to whom Foucault's research owes a theoretical debt he always acknowledged — argues that his description of the technologies of the self is too self-centered and that Foucault forgets that the purpose of the spiritual exercises is to overcome the self to act in concert with universal Reason. He says: "I can well understand Foucault's motives for giving short shrift to these aspects, of which he was perfectly aware. His description of the practices of the self — like, moreover, my description of spiritual exercises — is not merely an historical study, but rather a tacit attempt to offer contemporary mankind a model of life, which Foucault calls 'an aesthetics of existence'" (Hadot 1995, 208).
9. On this issue, see another passage of the interview with Deleuze: "No, there's definitely no return to the Greeks. Foucault hated returning anywhere. He only ever talked about what he himself was living through; and mastering oneself, or rather the production of self, speaks for itself in Foucault. What he says is that the Greeks 'invented' subjectivation, and did so because their social system, the rivalry between free men, made this possible (in games, oratory, love . . . and so on" (Deleuze 1995, 114).
10. Foucault 2011, p. 45. Foucault argues that the richness and fecundity of this notion arise not only from its versatility and plurality of semantic nuances, but also from its "longevity" and from the great ambiguity that surrounds it, because its general valorization is far from having been always constant and homogeneous. It is, in fact, a hardly studied notion, because — in spite of its numerous occurrences from the classical era until the Church Fathers

of the fifth century AD — it has never been expressly thematized, except for the largely lost treatise by Philodemus, a first century AD Epicurean. With the exception of a dubious fragment by Democritus, *parrhēsia* appears in Euripides and Aristophanes in a legal meaning. It designates the right of Athenian citizens to speak at assemblies and to participate in the political and legal life of the city. Over time, the meaning of the term widens as it moves from the public to the private sphere and acquires an increasingly moral connotation of frankness and courage in speaking. *Parrhēsia* turns more and more into the virtue required from the teacher, from the director of conscience, from the friend (Plato, Gorgias).

11. In *The Hermeneutics of the Subject*, Foucault continues his analysis by attempting a positive outline of *parrhēsia*. First, he analyzes a text by Philodemus to illustrate "an institutional image of the game of *parrhēsia*" in the Epicurean context. In Epicurean circles, *parrhēsia* is exercised both vertically by the director of consciousness — who must be in principle "dynastically" traced back to Epicurus — to the disciples, and horizontally in the friendship relationships within the group. Additionally, the students have an obligation to speak (to say what they think, what they care about, but also which faults they committed), which Foucault recognizes as the first foundation of what Christianity will transform into confession (Foucault 2005, 386–91). Secondly, he dwells on Galen's treatise on the passions (Foucault 2005, 395–400) and, finally, on Seneca's letters (40; 38; 29; 75) to Lucilius (Foucault 2005, 401–09).

12. See chapter 3.

13. *Parrhēsia* contrasts sharply with flattery, which is a rather complex dialectical procedure that those who are inferior deploy to obtain the benevolence of those who exercise power over them. On the one hand, the flatterers use language to obtain what they want from their superior, yet leveraging their superiority ends up reinforcing it. On the other hand, however, by preventing those who are flattered from knowing themselves for what they are and giving them a false self-image, flattery weakens them and makes them dependent on the flatterers.

14. *Parrhēsia* contrasts sharply with rhetoric, which is the art of persuasion based on a craft [*tekhnē*] specifying the rules needed to construct a discourse that would fit the argument at stake and would result in actions over the other producing the greatest advantage for the speaker.

15. For a thorough and insightful analysis of Foucault's reading of *parrhēsia*, see Lorenzini (2023). Relying on J. L. Austin and Stanley Cavell, Lorenzini suggests the speech act of *parrhēsia* from the perspective of its perlocutionary effect and he identifies seven conditions that characterize it: (1) unpredictability of the effect of the utterance; (2) freedom of the speaker; (3) criticism of the *ēthos* of the interlocutor(s); (4) indeterminate risk taken by the speaker; (5) courage shown by the speaker; (6) transparency of the utterance; (7) alethurgy — manifestation of the truth as an ethico-political force (89).

16. See Rancière (1987).
17. Lorenzini aptly notices that "in order to depict Socrates as a paradigmatic parrhesiastic figure, Foucault ends up downplaying the importance of what likely constitutes the most famous form that his discourse takes: irony [. . .] In short, when he uses irony, Socrates does not speak as a parrhesiast" (77).
18. Interestingly, Giuseppe Scarpat underlines how the need to coin the term *parrhēsia* "can only be explained by the desire to bring the emphasis on the act of 'saying,' an aspect so dear to the Greeks, as we said, while *isegoria* accentuated the concept of equality as all compounds of iso- do" (2001, 35).
19. See Foucault (2011, pp. 7–39); Foucault (1984, pp. 32–50); and Foucault (2003, pp. 263–78).
20. See previous sections in this chapter.
21. The Tokyo lecture "The Analytic Philosophy of Politics" dates from 27 April 1978 (Foucault 1978), while "What Is Critique?" was delivered on 27 May of the same year (Foucault 2003, 263–78).
22. See "What Is Critique?" (Foucault 2003, p. 266). On this issue, see Butler (2002, pp. 223–24), Deutscher (2017a, 207–31), Malabou (2023, 113–43), and Villalobos-Ruminott 2022.
23. In the lecture "What Is critique?" Foucault differentiates Enlightenment and critique as an attitude opposed to instances of governmentalization from Kant's three Critiques. The latter inaugurate the tradition of analysis as an inquiry into the legitimacy of historical knowledge, which is generally what Enlightenment is reduced to and which is the main reference of philosophers such as Dilthey and Habermas (see Foucault 2003, p. 273).

Afterword

1. "This is the *parrhēsiastic* discourse and standpoint in philosophy: it is the discourse of the irreducibility of truth, power, and *ēthos*, and at the same time the discourse of their necessary relationship, of the impossibility of thinking truth [*alētheia*], power [*politeia*], and *ēthos* without their essential, fundamental relationship to each other." (Foucault 2009, 68)
2. See Lorenzini, 37–40.
3. In regard to the notion of *infrapolitical* that I am using here, see as references, among others, Cerrato 2015, Cerrato Backer 2025, Mendoza de Jesus 2015, Moreiras 2021 and 2022, Rodriguez-Matos 2015, Villalobos-Ruminott 2015, Williams 2021.

Bibliography

Álvarez Yágüez, Jorge. *Michel Foucault: Verdad, Poder, Subjetividad. La Modernidad Cuestionada*. Ed. Pedagógicas, 1995.

Bennington, Geoffrey. *Scatter 1: The Politics of Politics in Foucault, Heidegger, and Derrida*. Fordham UP, 2016.

Bernini, Lorenzo. *Le Pecore e Il Pastore. Critica, Politica, Etica Nel Pensiero Di Michel Foucault*. Liguori, 2008.

Berti, Enrico. *Aristotele Nel Novecento*. Laterza, 1992.

———. "Il Metodo Della Filosofia Pratica Secondo Aristotele." *Studi Sull'etica Di Aristotele*, edited by Antonina Alberti, Bibliopolis, pp. 23–63.

Bodei, Remo. "Foucault: Pouvoir Politique et Maîtrise de Soi." *Critique*, 471–72, 1986, pp. 898–917.

Brindisi, Gianvito. *Potere e Giudizio. Giurisdizione e Veridizione Nella Genealogia Di Michel Foucault*. Editoriale scientifica, 2010.

Brown, Wendy. "Genealogical Politics." *The Later Foucault*, edited by Jeremy Moss, Sage, 1998, pp 33–49.

Butler, Judith. *Giving an Account of Oneself*. Fordham UP, 2005.

———. "What Is Critique? An Essay on Foucault's Virtue." *The Political*, edited by David Ingram, Blackwell, 2002, pp. 212–26.

Caruso, Paolo. "Who Are You, Professor Foucault? (Interview)." *Religion and Culture*, edited by James Carrette, translated by Lucille Cairns, Manchester UP, 1999, pp 87–103.

Castel, Robert. "Les Aventures de la Pratique." *Le Débat*, 41, 1986, pp. 41–51.

Catucci, Stefano. *Introduzione a Foucault*. Laterza, 2020.

Cerrato, Maddalena. "Infrapolitics and Shibumi: Infrapolitical Practice Between and Beyond Metaphysical Closure and End of History." *Transmodernity* vol. 5, no.1, 2015, pp. 81–105.

Cerrato, M., and P. Baker. "Autographic Praxis: An Infrapolitical Adventure" *Angelaki: Journal of the Theoretical Humanities* 30.6, 2025.

Cremonesi, Laura. "La Tragédie d'œdipe dans l'œuvre de Foucault." *Cahiers Parisiens*, 2005, pp. 275–94.

Davidson, Arnold I. "Archaeology, Genealogy, Ethics." *Foucault: A Critical Reader*, edited by David Couzens Hoy, Blackwell, 1986, pp. 221–34.

Del Re, Antonio. *L'etica Tra Felicità e Dovere*. Edizioni Dehoniane Bologna, 1986.

———. "Figure Dell'etica." *Introduzione All'etica*, edited by Carmelo Vigna, Vita e Pensiero, 2001, pp. 3–117.

Deleuze, Gilles. *Foucault*. Translated by Sean Hand, U Minnesota P, 1988.

———. *Negotiations, 1972–1990*. Edited by Michael Joughin, Columbia UP, 1995.

———. *Pourparlers. 1972–1990*. Minuit, 1990.

———. *Pure Immanence: Essays on a Life*. Translated by Anne Boyman, Zone Books, 2001.

Derrida, Jacques. "'To Do Justice to Freud': The History of Madness in the Age of Psychoanalysis." Translated by Pascale-Anne Brault and Michael Naas. *Critical Inquiry*, vol. 20, no. 2, 1994, pp. 227–66.

Deutscher, Penelope. "The Critical Time of the Present." *Critical Theory in Critical Times: Transforming the Global Political and Economic Order*, edited by P. Deutscher and C. Lafont, Columbia UP, 2017a, pp. 207–31.

———. *Foucault's Futures: A Critique of Reproductive Reason*. Columbia UP, 2017b.

Dreyfus, Hubert L., and Paul Rabinow. *Michel Foucault. Beyond Structuralism and Hermeneutics*. Chicago UP, 1982.

Elden, Stuart. *Foucault's Last Decade*. Polity Press, 2016.

Eribon, Didier. *Michel Foucault: 1926–1984*. Translated by Betsy Wing, Harvard UP, 1991.

Erlenbusch-Anderson, Verena. *Genealogies of Terrorism*, Columbia UP, 2018.

Ewald, François, Annette Farge, and Michelle Perrot. "Une Pratique de la Vérité." *Michel Foucault: Une Histoire de la Vérité*, edited by Robert Badinter, Syros, 1995, pp. 9–18.

Faustino, M., and G. Ferraro. "Introduction: Another Word on Foucault's Final Words." *The Late Foucault: Ethical and Political Questions*, edited by M. Faustino and G. Ferraro, Bloomsbury Academic, 2020, pp. 1–18.

Flynn, Thomas R. "Truth and Subjectivation in the Later Foucault." *The Journal of Philosophy*, 82, October 1985, pp. 531–40.

Fontana, Alessandro. "Leggere Foucault, Oggi." *Foucault, Oggi*, edited by Mario Galzigna, Feltrinelli, 2008, pp. 29–44.

Foucault, Michel. *Abnormal: Lectures at the Collège de France, 1974–1975*. Edited by Valerio Marchetti and Antonella Salomoni. Translated by Graham Burchell, Palgrave MacMillan, 2007a.

———. *About the Beginning of the Hermeneutics of the Self: Lectures at Dartmouth College, 1980*. Edited by Henri-Paul Fruchaud, Daniele Lorenzini, Laura Cremonesi, Arnold I. Davidson, Orazio Irrera, and Martina Tazzioli. Translated by Graham Burchell, U Chicago P, 2016a.

———. *Aestetics, Method, and Epistemology*. Edited by James D. Faubion. New Press, 1998b.

―――. "The Analytic Philosophy of Politics [Gendai No Kenryoku Wo Tou]." Translated by Giovanni Mascaretti. *Foucault Studies*, June 1978d, pp. 188–200.

―――. *Les Anormaux. Cours au Collège de France. 1974–1975*. Edited by Valerio Marchetti and Antonella Salomoni. Seuil-Gallimard, 1999.

―――. *The Birth of Biopolitics: Lectures at the Collège de France, 1978–1979*. Edited by Michel Senellart. Translated by Graham Burchell, Palgrave MacMillan, 2010.

―――. *The Birth of Clinic : An Archaeology of Medical Perception*. Translated by Alan Sheridan Smith, Vintage Books, 1994c.

―――. *Bisogna Difendere La Società*. Edited by Mauro Bertain and Alessandro Fontana, Feltrinelli, 1998a.

―――. *The Care of the Self. Vol. 3: The History of Sexuality*. Vintage, 1988b.

―――. *The Courage of Truth: The Government of Self and Others II; Lectures at the Collège de France, 1983–1984*. Edited by Frédéric Gros. Translated by Graham Burchell, Palgrave MacMillan, 2012b.

―――. *Le Courage de la Vérité. Le Gouvernement de Soi et des Autres II. Cours au Collège de France. 1984*. Edited by Frédéric Gros under the direction of François Ewald et Alessandro Fontana, Seuil-Gallimard, 2009.

―――. "The Crisis of Medicine or the Crisis of Antimedicine?" *Foucault Studies* 1, 2004c, pp. 5–19.

―――. "Dialogue on Power." *Chez Foucault*, edited by Simeon Wade, Circabook, 1978a, pp. 4–22.

―――. *Discipline and Punish: The Birth of the Prison*. Translated by Alan M. Sheridan, Pantheon Books, 1978b.

―――. "The Discourse on Language." *The Archaeology of Knowledge*, by Michel Foucault, translated by Rupert Sawyer, Routledge, 2013c, pp. 215–37.

―――. *Dits et Écrits, 1954–1988*. Tome 2: 1970–1975. Gallimard, 1994a.

―――. *Dits et Écrits, 1954–1988*. Tome 4: 1980–1988. Gallimard, 1994b.

―――. *Ethics: Subjectivity and Truth*. Edited by Paul Rabinow. Translated by Robert Hurley, New Press, 1997a.

―――. *The Essential Foucault*. Edited by Paul Rabinow and Nikolas Rose, New Press, 2003c.

―――. *Foucault Live! (Interviews, 1966–1984)*. Edited by Sylvère Lotringer. Semiotext(e), 1996.

―――. *The Foucault Reader*. Edited by Paul Rabinow, Pantheon Books, 1984.

―――. *Le Gouvernement de Soi et des Autres. Cours au Collège de France 1982–1983*. Edited by Frédéric Gros, Seuil-Gallimard, 2008.

———. *Du Gouvernement des Vivants. Cours au Collège de France. 1979–1980.* Edited by Michel Senellart, Seuil-Gallimard, 2012a.

———. *The Government of Self and Others: Lectures at the College de France, 1982–1983.* Edited by Frédéric Gros. Translated by Graham Burchell, Palgrave MacMillan, 2011b.

———. *The Hermeneutics of the Subject: Lectures at the Collège de France, 1981–1982.* Edited by Frédéric Gros. Translated by Graham Burchell, Palgrave MacMillan, 2005.

———. *L'herméneutique du Sujet: Cours au Collège de France (1981–1982).* Edited by Frédéric Gros, Seuil-Gallimard, 2001b.

———. *History of Madness.* Translated by Jonathan Murphy and Jean Khalfa, Routledge, 2006b.

———. *The History of Sexuality. Vol. I: An Introduction.* Translated by Robert Hurley, Pantheon Books, 1978c.

———. *"Il Faut Défendre la Société": Cours au Collège de France (1975–1976).* Edited by Mauro Bertani and Alessandro Fontana, Seuil-Gallimard, 1997b.

———. "The Incorporation of the Hospital into Modern Technology." *Space, Knowledge and Power: Foucault and Geography*, edited by Stuart Elden and Jeremy W. Crampton, translated by Edgar Knowlton Jr., William J. King, and Stuart Elden, Ashgate, 2007c, pp. 141–52.

———. "Interview with Michel Foucault." *Power. Essential Works of Foucault, 1954–1984*, by Michel Foucault, edited by James D. Faubion, New Press, 2001a, pp 239–97.

———. *Leçons sur la Volonté de Savoir. Cours au Collège de France (1970–1971). Suivi de Le Savoir d'oedipe.* Seuil-Gallimard, 2011a.

———. *Lectures on the Will to Know: Lectures at the Collège de France, 1975–1976, with Oedipal Knowledge.* Edited by Daniel Defert. Translated by Graham Burchell, Palgrave MacMillan, 2013b.

———. "The Meshes of Power." *Space, Knowledge and Power: Foucault and Geography*, edited by Stuart Elden and Jeremy W. Crampton, translated by Gerald Moore, Ashgate, 2007d, pp. 153–62.

———. *Naissance de la Biopolitique. Cours au Collège de France. 1978–1979.* Edited by Michel Senellart, édition établie sous la direction de François Ewald and Alessandro Fontana, Seuil-Gallimard, 2004a.

———. "On the Genealogy of Ethics: An Overview of Work in Progress." *Ethics: Subjectivity and Truth*, by Michel Foucault, edited by Paul Rabinow, translated by Robert Hurley, New Press, 1997c, pp. 253–80.

———. *On the Government of the Living: Lectures at the Collège de France, 1979–1980.* Edited by Michel Senellart. Translated by Graham Burchell, Palgrave MacMillan, 2016b.

———. *The Order of Things*. Pantheon Books, 1970.

———. *Penal Theories and Institutions: Lectures at the Collège de France, 1971–1972*. Edited by Bernard E. Harcourt. Translated by Graham Burchell, Palgrave MacMillan, 2019.

———. *Le Pouvoir Psychiatrique. Cours Au Collège de France 1973–1974*. Edited by Jacques Lagrange, Seuil-Gallimard, 2003a.

———. *Power. Essential Works of Foucault, 1954–1984*. Edited by James D. Faubion, New Press, 2001c.

———. *Power/Knowledge: Selected Interviews and Other Writings, 1972–1977*. Edited by Colin Gordon, Pantheon Books, 1980.

———. *Psychiatric Power: Lectures at the Collège de France, 1973–1974*. Edited by Jacques Lagrange. Translated by Graham Burchell, Palgrave MacMillan, 2006a.

———. *The Punitive Society: Lectures at the Collège de France, 1972–1973*. Edited by Bernard Harcourt. Translated by Graham Burchell, Palgrave MacMillan, 2018.

———. *Sécurité, Territoire, Population. Cours au Collège de France. 1977–1978*. Edited by Michel Senellart, Seuil-Gallimard, 2004b.

———. *Security, Territory, Population: Lectures at the College de France, 1977–1978*. Edited by Michel Senellart. Translated by Graham Burchell, Palgrave MacMillan, 2007b.

———. "Sexuality and Power." *Les Anormaux. Cours au Collège de France. 1974–1975*, by Michel Foucault, edited by Valerio Marchetti and Antonella Salomoni, Seuil-Gallimard, 1999, pp. 115–30.

———. *La Société Punitive. Cours au Collège de France. 1972–1973*. Edited by Bernard E. Harcourt, Seuil-Gallimard, 2013a.

———. *Society Must Be Defended: Lectures at the Collège de France, 1975–1976*. Edited by Alessandro Fontana, David Macey, François Ewald, and Mauro Bertani, St. Martins Press, 2020.

———. *"Society Must Be Defended": Lectures at the Collège de France, 1975–1976*. Edited by Mauro Bertani and Alessandro Fontana. Translated by David Macey, Palgrave MacMillan, 2003b.

———. "The Subject and Power." *Michel Foucault. Beyond Structuralism and Hermeneutics*, edited by Hubert L. Dreyfus and Paul Rabinow, Chicago UP, 1982, pp. 208–26.

———. *Subjectivité et Vérité. Cours au Collège de France. 1980–1981*. Edited by Frédéric Gros, Seuil-Gallimard, 2014.

———. *Subjectivity and Truth: Lectures at the Collège de France, 1980–1981*. Edited by F. Gros. Translated by G. Burchell, Palgrave MacMillan, 2017.

———. *Technologies of the Self: A Seminar with Michel Foucault*. Edited by Luther H. Martin, Huck Guttman, and Patrick H. Hutton, U Massachusetts P, 1988a.

———. *Théories et Institutions Pénales. Cours au Collège de France (1971–1972)*. Edited by Bernard E. Harcourt, Seuil-Gallimard, 2015.

———. "Truth and Power." *Power. Essential Works of Foucault, 1954–1984*, by Michel Foucault, edited by James D. Faubion, New Press, 2001d, pp. 111–33.

———. *The Use of Pleasures*. Edited by Paul Rabinow and N. Rose. Vol. 2. *The History of Sexuality*. Vintage Books, 1990.

Gros, Frédéric. "Sujet Moral et Soi Éthique Chez Foucault." *Archives de Philosophie*, vol. 65, no. 2, 2002, pp. 229–37.

Hadot, Pierre. *Philosophy as a Way of Life: Exercises from Socrates to Foucault*. Edited by Arnold I. Davidson. Translated by Michael Chase, Blackwell, 1995.

Heidegger, Martin. *Pathmarks*. Edited by William McNeill, Cambridge UP, 1998.

———. "The Origin of the Work of Art." *Off the Beaten Track*, translated by Julian Young, Cambridge UP, 2002, pp. 1–56.

Islekel, Ege Selin. "Foucault and the Biopolitics of the Penitentiary." *The Biopolitics of Punishment: Derrida and Foucault*, edited by Rick Elmore and Ege Selin Islekel, Northwestern UP, 2022, pp. 71–86.

Janicaud, Dominique. "Rationality, Force, and Power: Foucault and Habermas's Criticism." *Michel Foucault. Philosopher*, edited by Timothy J. Armstrong, Harvester Wheatsheaf, 1992, pp. 283–302.

Kelly, Mark G. E. "Foucault, Subjectivity, and the Technology of the Self." *A Companion to Foucault*, edited by Christopher Falzon, Timothy OLeary, and Jana Sawicki, Wiley-Blackwell, 2013.

Le Blanc, Guillaume, and Jean Terrel. "Foucault au Collège de France: Un Itinéraire." *Michel Foucault au Collège de France: Un Itinéraire*, edited by Guillaume le Blanc and Jean Terrel, Presses Universitaires de Bordeaux, 2003, pp. 7–26.

Lorenzini, Daniele. *The Force of Truth: Critique, Genealogy, and Truth-Telling in Michel Foucault*. U of Chicago P, 2023.

Luce, Sandro. *Fuori Di Sé: Poteri e Soggettivazioni in Michel Foucault*. Mimesis, 2009.

Lynch, R. A. *Foucault's Critical Ethics*. Fordham UP, 2016.

Malabou, Catherine. *Stop the Thief: Anarchism and Philosophy*. Polity Press, 2023.

McGushin, Edward F. *Foucault's Askesis: An Introduction to the Philosophical Life*. Northwestern UP, 2007.

Mendoza de Jesús, Ronald. "Sovereignty: An Infrapolitical Question." *Transmodernity*, 5 no.1, 2015, pp. 52–80.

Montinari, Moreno. *Foucault e Hadot Nello Specchio Dei Greci*. Mimesis, 2009.

Moreiras, Alberto. *Infrapolitics: A Handbook*. First edition, Fordham University Press, 2021.

———. *Uncanny Rest: For Antiphilosophy*. Translated by Camila Moreiras, Duke University Press, 2022.

Nilson, Herman. *Michel Foucault and the Games of Truth*. St. Martin's Press, 1998.

Pacchiani, Claudio, editor. *Filosofia Pratica e Scienza Politica*. Francisci, 1980.

Palazzo, Giovanni Antonio. *Discorso Del Governo e Della Ragion Vera Di Stato*. Giovanni Battista Sottili, 1604.

Pandolfi, Alessandro. "La 'Natura' Della Popolazione." *Governare La Vita: Un Seminario Sui Corsi Di Michel Foucault Al Collège de France, 1977–1979*, edited by Sandro Chignola, Ombre corte, 2006, pp. 91–116.

———. *Tre Studi Su Foucault*. Terzo millennio, 2000.

Rancière, Jacques. *Le Maître Ignorant*. Fayard, 1987.

Rayner, Timothy. "Foucault, Heidegger, and the History of Truth." *Foucault and Philosophy*, edited by Timothy O'Leary and Christopher Falzon, Wiley-Blackwell, 2010, pp. 60–77.

Revel, Judith. *Foucault. Un'ontologia Dell'attualità*. Rubettino, 2003.

Rodriguez-Matos, Jaime. "Nihilism and the Deconstruction of Time: Notes Toward Infrapolitics." *Transmodernity*, vol. 5, no.1, 2015, pp. 36–51.

Rovatti, Pier Aldo. "Il soggetto che non c'è." *Foucault, Oggi*, edited by Mario Galzigna, Feltrinelli, 2008, pp. 216–25.

Scarpat, Giuseppe. *Parrhesia Greca, Parrhesia Cristiana*. Paideia, 2001.

Schürmann, Reiner. *Heidegger on Being and Acting: From Principles to Anarchy*. Indiana UP, 1984.

———. "On Constituting Oneself as an Anarchist Subject." *Praxis International*, vol. 6, no. 3, 1986, pp. 294–310.

Sheridan, Alan. *Michel Foucault: The Will to Truth*. Tavistock, 1980.

Sluga, Hans. "Foucault's Encounter with Heidegger and Nietzsche." *The Cambridge Companion to Foucault*, edited by Gary Gutting, Cambridge UP, 2005, pp. 210–39.

———. "'I Am Simply a Nietzschean.'" *Foucault and Philosophy*, edited by Timothy O' Leary and Christopher Falzon, Wiley-Blackwell, 2010, pp. 36–59.

Sorman, Guy. *Mon dictionnaire du bullshit*. Grasset, 2021.

Villalobos-Ruminott, Sergio. "El poema de la universidad:nihilismo e infrapolítica." *Transmodernity*, vol. 5, no.1, 2015, pp. 106–22.

———. "Foucault: Archeologia e Anarchia." *Laboratorio di Archeologia Filosofica*, 2022, pp.1–23.

Volpi, Franco. "La Riabilitazione Della Filosofia Pratica Ed Il Suo Senso Nella Crisi Della Modernità." *Il Mulino*, vol. 35, no. 6, 1986, pp. 928–49.

Williams, Gareth. *Infrapolitical Passages: Global Turmoil, Narco-Accumulation, and the Post-Sovereign State*. Fordham University Press, 2021.

Zanini, Adelino. "Invarianza Neoliberale. Foucault e l'economia Politica." *Governare La Vita: Un Seminario Sui Corsi Di Michel Foucault Al Collège de France, 1977–1979*, edited by Sandro Chignola, Ombre corte, 2006, pp. 117–52.

Index

Abnormal, 41, 44
alethurgy, 71, 119–20n7, 123n15
anarchaeology, 30, 32
anarchaeogenealogy, 14–15, 28, 30, 32, 35, 40–41, 82, 84, 86, 90, 104–06
anarchy, principle of, 16, 23, 25, 29–31, 104
antiquity, 75, 82, 84–86, 90, 92–94, 98
archaeology, 20, 22, 24–25, 27, 105, 114n15
arché, 16, 25, 30, 114n15
archive, 25–26, 107, 111n5, 114n15
Aristotle, 14, 30–31, 37, 49, 98, 115n22
asceticism, 87–89
autonomy, 10, 15, 29, 68, 95, 102, 105; autonomous subjectivation, 15, 17, 31–32, 34, 37, 75, 79, 81, 83–84, 90–92, 99–101, 106, 109. *See also* subjectivation

biopolitics, 36, 48–54, 57, 65–67, 76, 116n8, 117n10–11
biopower, 3–4, 12–13, 20, 48–53, 66–67, 70, 116n2, 117n11
Butler, Judith, 34–36, 110, 111n3, 115n25, 117n10, 124n22

care, of the self, 28, 76–77, 79, 83–90, 91, 93, 97, 121n6, 122n7
Christianity, 22, 66, 69, 71–75, 84–85, 87, 89, 120n9, 123n11. *See also* pastoral
Confession, 51, 66–67, 70–75, 119n2, 120–21n12, 123n11

conduct, 28, 33, 69, 71, 77, 79, 82, 85–86, 90, 91, 103, 118n24. *See also ēthos*
contingency, 23, 25–26, 30–31, 94, 105–06, 108–09
Clausewitz, 47, 116n7
Courage of Truth, The, 83, n111
critique, 1, 14, 17, 29–32, 35, 99, 101–06, 108–09, 112n12, 115n16, 124n23
Cynic, 109, 122n7

death, 49, 50, 73, 94, 117n11, 121n13
Deleuze, Gilles, 1–2, 4–5, 6, 10–11, 14–15, 19, 31–32, 34–35, 39, 65, 81, 82, 84–86, 107, 111n5, 112n10–11, 113n3, 115n1, 121n1, 122n9
déplacement, 10, 52, 65–66, 78–79, 81
Derrida, Jacques, 5, 110
Descartes, René, 21, 87; Cartesian, 22, 87
Deutscher, Penelope, 109–110, 117n10, 124n22
discipline, 42–43, 48–51, 53–56
Discipline and Punish, 9, 41, 46, 49, 121n5
discourse, 2, 22, 24–27, 41, 46–48, 51, 54, 67, 73, 87, 92–96, 98–99, 102, 105–06, 119n2, 123n14, 124n17, 124n1; discursive practice, 27, 41, 73, 82, 108
domination, 15, 23, 33, 43, 46–47, 76–77, 81–84, 108
Dreyfus, Hubert, 3, 6, 12–13, 20, 26, 30, 46, 70, 85, 90, 113n16, 121n5. *See also* Rabinow, Paul

economy, 46, 51, 53–54, 56, 58, 60–61, 109
emancipation, 1, 15, 33, 96–97, 99, 104–105, 108–110
Enlightenment, 102, 104–106, 124n23
exercises, 35–36, 77, 84, 86, 89, 96, 122n7, 122n8
ethics, 14, 27, 29, 36–37, 78, 93–95, 113n17, 121n5; Ancient/Classical, 82, 84, 86, 88–91; Christian, 89; *ēthos*, 16, 28–29, 33, 35–37, 77, 86, 91–92, 95–97, 99, 102–03, 105–08, 123n15, 124n1; *ēthopoiesis*, 79, 95; Greek, 85, 90; as one of the three axes of experience (knowledge, power, ethics), 14, 32, 106; of care of the self, 83, 89–90; as self-relationship (relationship with themselves), 24, 28,82, 85, 95
existence, 14, 17, 22, 45, 49–50, 57–58, 62, 68, 82, 86, 90, 92, 98, 101–02, 107–10, 113n17, 122n8
exagoreusis, 74, 120n9
exomologesis, 73–74, 120n9, 121n13
experience, 31–32, 43, 81–82, 87–88, 101, 105–10; dimensions/axes of, 17, 27–28, 32–33, 82, 91, 106 forms of, 30; of freedom, 27, 90, 110; religious, 92

force, 15–16, 35, 39, 43, 47, 79, 91, 108–109, 116n7, 123n15
freedom, 1, 16, 17, 27, 31, 33, 44, 47, 59, 62, 66, 69, 83–84, 93–94, 98, 105, 110, 118n21, 123n15; as autonomy/autonomous subjectivation, 17, 79, 84–85, 109; ēthos–poietic, 33, 36, 84, 95; exercise or practice of, 15–16, 28–29, 33–35, 37, 76, 95–96, 99, 101, 103, 109; of individuals, 81, 85, 90; as resistance, 33, 77; -security, 59–60, 62
Freud, Sigmund, 45, 114n11, 116n4

game of truth, 21, 25, 27, 40
genealogy, 4, 13, 20–21, 24–27, 56, 65, 70, 72, 76, 84, 105, 109, 115n28, 121n5
GIP (*Groupe d'information sur les prisons*) 9, 46
Government of Self and Others, The, 83, 92, 97, 104, 108
government, 29, 49, 52, 54–58, 60–63, 66, 68, 70–71, 77–79, 83, 88, 91–93, 104, 108–09, 117n14; of others, 29, 33, 83, 108; self-/ of the self, 29, 34, 56, 83–84, 108; of truth, 17, 40, 65–66, 76, 81–84, 87, 91–92, 97, 99; of men by the truth, 17, 28, 68, 76, 78, 91, 102
governmentality, 34, 39, 52, 54–55, 57, 59–63, 66–71, 75–78, 81–83, 93, 98, 102, 116n2, 118n17, 118n20, 118n24

Hadot, Pierre, 36, 89, 122n7, 122n8
Heidegger, Martin, x, 11–13, 16, 29, 37, 87, 110, 112n13, 115n22, 120n7
hermeneutics, 72, 75, 84–86, 115n22
Hermeneutics of the Subject, The, 82–83, 85, 93, 123n11
heroism, 16, 37, 109
heteronomy, 16, 96, 109; heteronomous, 15, 28–29, 33–35, 67, 103, 106. *See also* subjectivation
historicity, 2, 15, 22–24, 30–31, 33, 101, 104, 108, 118n17
History of Madness, The, 27, 40–41, 44
History of Sexuality, The, 11, 41–42, 44, 46, 66, 85, 121n5
Homo oeconomicus, 60–62, 118n21–n22
human sciences, 22, 25, 72, 75, 82
Husserl, 20–21, 87

ideology, 22, 25, 27, 40, 78
individual, the, 25, 27–29, 35, 41, 43, 50, 60–61, 66–67, 69–70, 72, 75, 77, 84–85, 92, 96; individualization, 66, 70; individualizing, 34, 50, 67–68, 70, 75, 81

juridical, 32–33, 47, 62, 66–67, 77–78, 84–85, 89, 98

Kant, Immanuel, 22, 29, 104. *See also* Enlightment. *See also Was ist Aufklärung?*
Kehre (turning point), 10–11, 14, 17, 46, 70, 76, 79, 81
knowledge, 1, 21, 32, 41, 50, 61, 71–72, 74–75, 85, 95–97, 100, 104, 108, 122n7; *connaissance*, 25, 32; as first of the three axes/dimensions of experience, 14–15, 19, 32, 40, 106; formation of, 25, 82; power and, 12, 17, 19, 28, 34–35, 39–46, 48–49, 51–54, 57, 65–66, 76, 79, 81–82, 107, 115n2, 117n11; object(s) of, 23–25, 27, 55; self-knowledge, 34, 86, 87–89; subject(s) of, 25, 27, 87, 121n5
law, 22, 33, 36, 43–45, 47–49, 50, 56, 61, 69, 73, 83, 86–87, 89, 98, 100–01, 106
life, 33, 49–50, 62, 68, 73, 75, 89–90, 93, 99, 117n10–11, 121n13, 122n8, 123n10
liberalism, 51, 53, 57–59, 61–63
Lorenzini, Daniele, 27, 108, 115n17, 123n15, 124n17, 124n2

Malabou, C., 109–110, 124n22
Marxism, 20, 22–23, 26, 45–46, 53, 55, 88, 114n4, 114n11
modernity, 4, 22, 54–55, 59, 66–68, 70, 76, 85, 104, 116n6

morality, 22, 36, 66, 85–86, 89–90, 93

neoliberalism, 59–61
Nietzsche, Friedrich, 20, 26, 39, 47, 87, 104, 114n3, 118n1
norm, 16, 46, 50, 53; normal (vs abnormal), 44, 53, 119n2; normalization, 13, 44–45, 50, 53, 117n11

obedience, 56, 69–70, 74–75, 84, 91, 97, 102
obligation, 66–67, 71–72, 74–75, 86, 91, 123n11
Order of Things, The, 22, 27, 114n8, 121n5

parrhēsia, 16, 17, 29, 37, 76, 79, 82–83, 91–99, 100–05, 109, 123n10–15, 124n18; act, 94; *ēthos*, 37; parrhēsiast, 94–97, 109; parrhēsiastic, 96–97, 124n17, 124n1; model, 91; philosopher, 37; practice, 99
pastoral, 66, 68–69, 75, 85, 91, 97; care, 55–56, 65, 67–68, 70, 72, 84; power, 17, 34, 66, 67–70, 75, 91, 102, 118n1
philosophy: analytic, 5, 21, 104, 124n21; classical, 55, 75; of history, 14, 42, 48; moral, 89; political, 45, 55
practical. See practical philosophy
Plato, 37, 85, 88, 98, 100, 102, 119n4, 122n7, 123n10
police, 57, 61
politics: 8–9, 14, 32, 36–37, 46, 49, 61, 63, 68, 72, 83, 88, 92, 97–98, 100–03, 115n28, 116n6–7, 117n11; of ourselves, 72; of truth, 102
population, 49–50, 52–54, 56–58, 62–63, 67, 78, 11n2, 117n10–11, 117,13

power: biopolitical, 57; disciplinary, 42–43, 46, 49, 63, 116n3; modes of, 1, 78, 108–09; pastoral, 17, 34, 66, 68–70, 75, 91, 102, 118n1; psychiatric, 40–43; registers of, 1; -relationships; 12, 15, 23, 25, 27–28, 32–33, 41–42, 45, 47–49, 51, 54, 56, 63, 66, 75–78, 96, 98, 102, 106, 108, 114n14, 116n7, 119n2; repressive, 44, 66–67; as second axis/dimension of experience, 39–41; sovereign, 42–43, 49–50, 61, 69; theory of, 3, 23, 36, 40, 43, 46, 78, 107, 112n14, 113n16

power/knowledge. *See* knowledge

practice: ascetic, 32, 35; confessional, 72, 93; of freedom, 16, 28, 33, 35, 80, 84, 95, 99; *parrhēsiastic* practice, 99; philosophical, 28, 36, 95, 100–01; theory and, 13, 30, 103; of truth (Alethurgical –) 51, 79, 87, 92. *See also* alethurgy

practical philosophy, 1–2, 5, 14–16, 17, 19–20, 23, 28–33, 35–37, 39, 65–66, 72, 76, 79, 81– 82, 84, 100–01, 103–04, 106, 107–10

prince, 56, 99, 117n16

problematization, ix, 1, 5, 9, 42, 46, 62, 84, 86, 90, 91, 93, 101, 112n10. *See also* genealogy

psychoanalysis, 21, 88, 110

Rabinow, Paul, 3, 6, 12–13, 20, 26, 31, 46, 70, 85, 90, 113n16–17, 121n5. *See also* Dreyfus, Hubert

racism, 48, 117n11

raison d'État, 55–58, 60–62, 117n16

Rancière, Jacques, 96–97, 124n16

rationality, 57–58, 62, 66, 100, 106

regime of truth, 15–16, 27, 34–35, 37, 40, 42, 58–59, 62, 67, 71, 84, 92, 96, 101, 104, 109

resistance, 1, 15, 33, 35, 48, 72, 76–77, 79, 83, 101, 103, 108–09

security, 52–54, 57, 59–60, 62–63, 65, 67–68, 76

Security, Territory, Population, 52, 68, 76

sex, 12, 50–51,119n2

sexuality, 41–42, 44–45, 50–51, 62, 82, 112n10, 117n10–n11, 119n2. *See also History of Sexuality, The*

Schürmann, Reiner, 5, 14, 16, 34

Socrates, 88, 97, 124n17

Society Must Be Defended, 42, 44, 46–47, 49

spiritual, 3, 35, 74, 87–88; direction, 67; exercises, 36, 89, 122n8

state, 4, 8, 23, 35, 45, 47–48, 54–58, 60–62, 67, 77, 83, 114n11, 116n6, 117n11, 117n14, 117n16–17, 118n20; Modern state, 67–68

structuralism, 7, 12, 20–22, 26

submission, 43, 49, 69, 75, 84, 87

subject: constituent, 23–24, 30, 32, 57; issue of the, 3, 14, 16, 19–20; modern, 12, 21, 23, 30, 84; philosophy of the, 2, 5, 15, 20–22; subject–object, 25, 53; and truth, 40, 73, 87, 93

subjectivity, 6 14, 16–17, 20, 32–35, 41, 49, 50–51, 61–62, 72–74, 76–77, 79, 82, 84–85, 90–91, 95–96, 106, 114n3

subjection (assujettissement), 21, 29, 34, 41, 43, 84, 86, 89, 92, 109, 113n21

subjectivation: forms (or modes), 1, 12, 15, 27, 29, 32, 34, 60, 81, 85, 106–08; free/autonomous (*anarchical*), 16, 17, 31–35, 37, 75, 79, 81, 84, 87, 90–92, 96, 99–101, 105–06, 109; freedom of, 84–85; heteronomous, 29, 33–35, 67; philosophical, 108

techniques: disciplinary, 59, 65; of domination, 76; of examination, 70, 74; of government, 54–55, 84, 93; of the self, 29, 76–78, 81, 85, 89; of subjection, 92; of subjectivation, 70, 72
totalizing, 23, 34, 67, 70, 75, 81, 106. *See also* individualizing
truth: criterion/criteria of, 25, 58, 79; force of, 27, 108–09; games of, 24–25, 103; government of, 17, 40, 66, 76, 81–84, 87, 91–92, 97, 99; history of, 67; manifestation of, 71, 73, 91, 93, 97, 99, 123n15; practices of, 47, 51, 72, 76, 79, 87, 92, 95; regime(s) of, 15–16, 27, 33–35, 37, 40, 42, 58–59, 63, 67, 71, 79, 84, 92, 96, 101, 104, 108–09; truth-telling, 94, 98–101; universal, 48, 79, 107
turning point. See *Kehre*

Use of Pleasures, The, 42

veridiction, 59–60, 82, 93, 97. *See also* truth

war, 47–48, 116n6, 116n7
Was ist Aufklärung? 83, 102, 104. *See also* Enlightenment
will, 69, 74–75, 84, 104
Will to Know, The, 46, 48

www.ingramcontent.com/pod-product-compliance
Lightning Source LLC
Chambersburg PA
CBHW030556230426
43661CB00054B/2162